THE CROSSOVER

MIRIAM TAMAR HOLMES

My Scribe Publishing

Copyright © 2023 by Miriam Tamar Holmes

All rights reserved.

No part of this book may be reproduced in any form or by any electronic or mechanical means, including information storage and retrieval systems, without written permission from the author, except for the use of brief quotations in a book review.

ISBN: 978-1-7379354-3-8

CONTENTS

Foreword — v
Acknowledgments — xiii
Author's Note — xxi

Part One
FIRST QUARTER

1. Jump Ball — 3
   20 years before — 5
2. OUT-OF-BOUNDS — 17
3. Fast Break — 30
   Time-Out — 39

Part Two
SECOND QUARTER

4. AIR BALL — 45
5. BLOCK OUT — 54
6. REBOUND — 69

   Halftime — 79

Part Three
THIRD QUARTER

7. OUTSIDE SHOOTER	85
8. FOUL BALL	94
9. FREE THROW	100
Time-Out	109

Part Four
FOURTH QUARTER

10. HOME COURT ADVANTAGE	115
11. FULL COURT PRESS	124
12. CROSSOVER	131
Overtime Winning Affirmations	149
Footnote Citations	153

FOREWORD

Blessed are the pure in heart, for they shall see God. (Matthew 5:8 [KJV])

It is rare to meet a person that has gone through so many intricate twists and turns in life to still find a way to have submitted enough of themselves to God to be considered "pure in heart." When I first met Miriam upon her return back to her hometown and church, she had such a humility about herself, and she was so open to receive from God. She had one million questions, and I was not sure that just because I was the first lady of her church, I could answer them. She had me seeking God even more myself just to be able to keep up *with her inquiries. She began to follow me as I followed Christ, and she had an undeniable determination to grow in God, and grow is what she did.*

In her debut book THE CROSSOVER, Miriam shares her strong and heartfelt testimony of how she flourished by leaps and bounds despite the obstacles she encountered on her journey out of homosexuality and into holiness. She speaks and teaches with such wit and raw truth as she invites us into the most intimate areas of her walk toward and, sometimes away from God. We get to vicariously experience life in Miriam's shoes in a way that validates her authenticity and her credibility. Throughout the chapters of this book, Miriam gives us her real-time experiences in such a profound way, that we can encourage others to win using anecdotes from her narrative.

Miriam keeps-it-VERY-real as she lays out how the enemy plotted and schemed to keep her in darkness, but how she fought her way to the light. I would dare say that this is a mature read, but the way this world is wired today, exposure to the brutal facts of life has to begin at an earlier stage now more than ever before. What better way to prepare those maturing youth, as well as those who may feel a call to minister to those in an alternative lifestyle than with a message as powerful as Miriam's? Whether you deliberately seek out this book or stumble upon it-you will certainly be blessed, equipped, and inspired by this memoir of transformation and change. You will cry and even burst at the seams with laughter at how Miriam's candid humor can find the bright side in even the most serious of issues.

THE CROSSOVER is an eye-opening read with relatability and transparency that will make an indelible cross-cultural, multi-generational mark for years to come. God will use both Miriam and this book to birth deliverance throughout the nations, and I'm soooo excited to be alive to see the way He will use Miriam and her testimony to make an explosive impact upon our world!

First Lady Malaika S. Howard
St. Mark Church (Mound Bayou, MS)

DEDICATION

IDA MAE & MURRAY NELSON

TO MY GRANDPARENTS

Mere words of thanks could NEVER come close to expressing how much you two mean to me. This book is FOR and BECAUSE of YOU BOTH. Let me explain just how much you have impacted my life.

Grandma, thank you for giving me the 23rd Number of Psalms. Psalms 23 taught me to walk in my authority in God even in the most difficult and darkest moments in life. It has also encouraged me that I don't have to be afraid of the enemy because Satan has been defeated. Psalms 23 reminds me of God's gentleness, love, and kindness for his children. It reminds me that He will always be my provider and my protector. No matter what I have gone through in life, You sharing God's word with me early helped me learn to trust the plan that God had for my life, because He really is the Good Shepherd!

Grandad, for as long as I could remember, I loved being around you so much! We were a team. You were truly the man. You were witty and you always had something strong and funny to share with me. You were kind to me and it was obvious to everyone that I was your absolute favorite. You were the first person to teach me how to drive a car and the first person to teach me how to ride a bike. You showed me how to change a flat tire and how to be fearless! Your love for your family has shown me what true love looks like. Thank you for favoring me like no other and believing in me!

Grandma, you had a building in our hometown called "The Prayer Temple" where many residents of Mound Bayou came to lay down their burdens in prayer and be led right to God's throne through your anointed prayers. You seemed to really have God's cell phone number! I remember that your favorite song was literally "Jesus is on the Mainline!" I can still hear your voice singing those words in my head. You could reach GOD HIMSELF like nobody's business! I remember your morning radio broadcast from the radio station WCLD in Cleveland, Mississippi that played every Sunday morning. That live broadcast was *truly your passion and you never missed a Sunday praying, singing and reading scriptures to the listeners. You were an example for my mother who is now an intercessor just like you were, and you set the stage for the ministry that God has so graciously given me as well. I'm beyond grateful for you grandma. Your love and passion for God still permeates our family to this very day. Your influence on my life and on our family has been so profound. Because of your light and love for Jesus Christ, I understand that God's Word is not just a part of life, but it has become the essence of life itself to me. I'm so thankful for the truths you shared with and imparted into me because they helped mold me into the woman of faith that I am becoming today.*

I will always love and honor you both and forever cherish your memory

ACKNOWLEDGMENTS

**To my Parents
Flora Mae and Leonard Cornelius Holmes**

I'm sooo super-thankful that God chose you both to be my parents in this lifetime! In a word, you are both two AMAZING individuals! You both are truly the epitome of righteousness. The Bible tells us to honor thy father and mother; which is the first commandment with promise (Ephesians 6:1-2). Momma, you are my Rock! You have been through so many things and I have seen the power of your dedication to God and your communion with Him in prayer rescue and deliver you in difficult times and also in our times of need as a family. Your example of loving Jesus Christ has helped mold me into becoming the best version of myself that I could possibly be. Your faith has held us ***all*** up at various times on our journey.

Dad, you are such an excellent Bible teacher. You are so intelligent and detailed, and your passion for God's Word is so inspiring. Thank you for teaching me His Word from a child. I truly honor you both, not only because of who you are and the position you both hold in my life, but because you have exemplified sanctification ever since I can remember. You both made it a habit to show love to people from all walks of life, and you don't discriminate in who you share the power of God's grace with. I pray that one day I will have a marriage as successful and as godly as yours. Thank you for raising me in the fear and the admonition of the Lord. It has been a gift to my life that could never, ever be replaced. I love you both so very dearly!

To my Godmother
Pastor Jeanette Dansby-Lyas

It has been an honor to have you in my life since I was a little girl. I grew up uncertain of knowing who I would become, but one thing I was certain about from the moment I met you was being your armor bearer. Although, I never knew what it really meant for me to follow you around and carry your things- I'm so grateful that I did because I found deliverance in your voice, in your testimony, in your love for Christ, and in your love for me. Wanting to follow you gave me the spirit of an armor-bearer and it showed me how to wait on others. You are a warrior and I will always be ready to help you carry your weapons into battle. Thank you for never giving up on me, for encouraging me, for praying for me, and for preparing me for this war that we call life. I love you immensely!

**To my best friend
Kutheria McKnight**

Thank you for a lifetime of amazing memories!!! I wouldn't trade them for anything! Thank you for being you and still being here in my life, loving and supporting me no matter what or how much I've changed. You exemplify the true meaning of friendship. I love you forever!

To my all-time favorite #30 Michellda Bradshaw

Thank you for your unfailing support and love. God has used you in so many ways to make my life better. You have been here for me unconditionally. Thank you for the many laughs, tears, and encouragement. It has meant the world to me to have you by my side through my journey of deliverance. Having you as my friend and sister in Christ is one of the best things that could ever happen to me. I love you forever!

To my forever First Lady Malaika Howard

Thank you for your leadership, mentorship, wisdom, sisterhood, being here for me always, and being the midwife that helped me birth this book out. I could have never taken this journey this way without you. Thank you for your labor during my darkest moments and spiritual transitions. Though my contractions were painful, you were there every step of the way, letting me squeeze your hand as I breathed through my ugliest hours. Because of you, I was able to push out something far greater than I could have ever imagined. Thank you for hearing the cries of this unborn child. I love you beyond words.

**To my former Pastor, Big Brother, and the Watchman on the Wall
Pastor John Howard**

Thank you for always showing loving concern for me, my family, and all that goes on in my life. You have been my teacher, preacher, and reacher since the moment that I gave my life to Christ. I've learned so much from you. You have been the light in my path on this journey of deliverance. Thank you for preparing me for growth and greater things. I love you dearly!

**To my current leaders
Apostle Jonathan and Prophetess Ashley Brown**

Prophetess Ashley Brown, my spiritual mother, you have the anointing of a shepherd. You protect the flock against anything and anyone that seeks to destroy. You are a great inspiration that exemplifies righteous and godly living to women as well as men. Thank you for setting such an amazing example of a true worshiper, intercessor, wife, and prophetess for us all. I'm beyond grateful for the EXTRA! It gives me great joy to know that we're breaking the devil's neck together in this season! Miriam loves you!

Apostle Jonathan Brown, my spiritual father, thank you for ministering so faithfully the love of God…not only with your words, but also with your actions and through your life. I remember my first visit to The Carpenter's Church. There was pure love and comfort there, but most importantly, everyone had a hunger and thirst after God's heart. Your wisdom has helped me to elevate to a next-level anointing. Your love for God's Word strengthens and encourages me daily. I appreciate and honor you for your support and devotion. Love you dearly!

**To my baby nieces
Jakyra Grant and Jada Holmes**

JaKyra and Jada, thank you for your role in the daily challenges of helping me learn how to train up a child. It's not a day that goes by that I'm not grateful for having you both in my life. You are Gwen's babies, but you are definitely my daughters as well. I thank God for blessing us both with your presence. Our bond is magical and it will never be broken. Continue to keep God first in everything that you do. I love you always!

**To the coldest, most talented, and best big brother in the world
Octavius Holmes**

Thank you for your amazing support and love. You brought out a beauty in me that I thought was impossible to ever see. I'll never forget my very first photoshoot. Ever since that day, I have been living and walking in the beauty that God used you to reveal to me. Thank you for making any day of the year feel like Christmas to me. One of the greatest gifts in the world is when God gave me you as a big brother. You are indeed the goat of many talents! I love you forever bruh, bruh!

AUTHOR'S NOTE

Never in a million years would I have imagined as I was going through my most difficult seasons, that God would one day trust me to share my story. On top of that, God has positioned me to become a bearer of the Good News of Jesus Christ. I was so deep in sin that I couldn't fathom that somehow, God could transform my mess into a message worthy to be heard. Here I am today, writing an introduction to my very first book! To say that I'm in awe would be an understatement.

God gave me the name for this book two years ago. I became pregnant with this baby at a time in my life when I didn't even know that God was placing a seed on the inside of me. All I knew is that I couldn't hide or sit on my deliverance. A shift started to take place within my heart and yet, I still didn't see this baby coming to life. I had so many complications during this process because the enemy had become threatened by my progress. I didn't need to know why the enemy was attacking me but that's who he is and what he does.

Although the devil was working triple time to destroy me, God's seed inside of me had already started to take root. Everyone saw my transformation, but they didn't know the many battles and steps that I had to take for a healthy delivery. God has kept me and He has brought me to a place of freedom and deliverance that has made every tear and heartache sooo worth it! I'm so glad to now see and experience the kind of peace and joy that is only found in the presence of God. Two years later, my baby is still alive. I was tormented for a testimony such as this!!!

Thank you for taking this journey with me. It means so much that you would spend your hard-earned money to support the vision that God has given me in sharing how His goodness has transformed my entire life. Expect to laugh, cry, pray, and even be set free as you go through the highs and lows of rejection, rebellion, lust, perversion, transformation, deliverance, healing, and joy right alongside me in this memoir. As you read, you may discover new ways to help encourage others and share with those in need as they go through and try to make it to the other side of life! Who knows...you may even gain a new appreciation for and understanding of my first love, the game of basketball. It is my most sincere hope that, after you have finished reading this book, you will be able to CROSSOVER and maintain a new sense of freedom as well. Please help me further my message and ministry by recommending this book to others and sharing it on your social media outlets. Thank you in advance, and may God forever bless you!

Part One
FIRST QUARTER
I WAS JUST A TOMBOY

"Don't let the fear of rejection cause you to lose direction."

~Miriam Tamar Holmes

1
JUMP BALL

A method of putting a basketball into play by tossing it into the air between two opponents who jump up and attempt to tap the ball to a teammate...

As in the beginning...

It was 12-12-12. This triple-digit date will only fall once in a lifetime. What an unbelievable day it was! I remember having a conversation with her the day before about the upcoming date and she said something like: "Let's make an amazing memory tomorrow!" The request that she made next literally blew me away! Marriage?!? I mean, I was truly happy with the state of my relationship. She was the love of my life and I **did** want to share every part of my existence with her. Being with her just felt right. At that point, I couldn't imagine life without her. I lived to make her happy, but for some reason, I couldn't shake the things my parents taught me. Honestly, the twelve years that I had lived an alternative lifestyle still never made marrying a woman feel like the right thing for me to do. Less than 24 hours later, I couldn't believe that we were headed to Iowa to get a same-sex marriage license! I was a nervous wreck, but I'd never felt love like this before in my entire life. This love was unconditional, everlasting, and authentic. It was strong enough to make me get out of the car and walk up to the courthouse door...

20 YEARS BEFORE

Let's go back and catch the replay of this particular game (my life). It all started at a very young age. For as long as I can remember, I was a tomboy. I never liked to wear dresses or skirts - not because they didn't look nice on me, but because I wanted to be comfortable. I don't ever remember enjoying jumping rope, dancing, or playing with dolls like some little girls do. Rather than play with my sister, I could always easily hang with my brothers or my cousins and have a good time just enjoying being outdoors. Again, I was literally just a tomboy who loved running, jumping, riding my bike, and playing outside. Enjoying the same things that my brothers enjoyed certainly didn't make me your average little girl, but this was not particularly odd in the 1980's either.

When I was younger, I remember that it was very important to my mom that my siblings and I looked nice. It was not second nature for me to worry about what clothes I put on, as I was only interested in getting to the fun my neighborhood and my friends had to offer! Consequently, I didn't develop a strong sentiment toward trying to "dress to impress" early on. I would even get frustrated when my mom seemed to obsess over how I looked and what I had on, I even remember EVERY single time she sent me to school in a skirt. I recall being so upset and in tears because I felt uncomfortable and ashamed.

Truth is, I didn't know how to be relaxed or "at ease" in my own body at the time. That made it that much easier for me to prefer being covered up versus wearing a skirt. Pants have always been my comfort zone, because they protected my legs and I felt literally covered when I had them on. It was so much easier to run and jump and do all those things I enjoyed doing with pants on as an innocent and growing young girl. I had no idea how far life and living would one day take what was very normal for me and turn it into something with a totally different meaning and experience altogether.

I eventually got tired of wearing those skirts and came up with a plan. One day I made up my mind that the next time mom sent me to school in a skirt, I would stuff pants in my backpack and run straight to the restroom to change clothes as soon as I hit the school grounds! I eventually realized that it was not only that my mother liked nice things, but that she could see the beauty in me and worked hard to preserve and enhance it even way back then. If Mom had known that the enemy would one day come hard and strong to attack my femininity, she probably would have made me wear a skirt every day! It would take more than a skirt or beautiful dress to reclaim it, and even today, I'm still carefully walking through a season of self-discovery. I'm learning how to love myself intentionally as I become comfortable with loving every part of the body that God gave me.

I remember my parents working and us having to go across the street to Grandma and Grandad's house. They babysat us until our parents made it back from work after school and in the summertime. My most vivid and memorable childhood moments ended with a steady dose and constant stream of God's Word. We could be outside playing in the dirt, riding bikes, or simply having fun talking trash with the other neighborhood kids…but, when it was time to come back inside the house, things began to shift for me, my siblings, and my cousins too! Waiting, but NOT patiently inside was my evangelistic grandmother. She loved the Word of God and she was in her element when she was reciting and rehearsing the scriptures. As a child, this is where the fun ended for me! However, if we wanted to live to see another day, my siblings, cousins and I had to learn every book of the Holy Bible from beginning to end! Along with engaging her in many other biblical activities, we literally had bible study at least three times a week. My time with grandma would not be complete if I didn't mention those **additional** prayer services that filled up the empty spaces in my young life without a whole lot of room left over for much else!

I remember my grandmother making us read and memorize the entire chapter of the Twenty-Third number of Psalms. As a child, I would quote scriptures and although I could hear them as I said them, I didn't understand what they meant at the time. Even then, God was using my grandmother. She was truly a force to be reckoned with in God's kingdom. She set a framework for our family that continues to this day. Her faith propelled me into my destiny.

In addition to being a tomboy, I was also a church kid! Not only was I a church kid, but I was actually a PREACHER'S KID (PK)! My parents had (and still have) a marriage that has been a very important part of my life. I did not come from a broken home, as they provided a stable environment and life for me and my siblings and modeled a long-lasting love. I have watched them serve God and His kingdom together all of my life. They do the work of the ministry, but I also grew up watching them be playful and loving at home *all* of the time.

I'm so thankful that my parents (and my grandmother) trained me up in the way I should go (Proverb 22:6 KJV), because it gave me something to return to when life got difficult. It might have seemed like I was ignoring their wisdom, but I could hear my parents' voices at various stages and in many scenarios while I was not saved. I believe it was the work of God's wisdom that kept me when both my life and my soul were involved in many dangerous situations.

My mom truly personifies love in every area of my life! She has been my rock and my biggest supporter since day one. She is a prayer warrior (just like her mother/my grandmother was) and has stood faithful on the post praying and interceding for me throughout every challenge regarding my identity and even alongside my choice to engage in a lifestyle of sin.

I can remember when I was fully immersed in "the lifestyle" and I would come home from a night of clubbing and drinking. Mom would literally "blow my high" quoting scriptures when she called me on the phone. I remember this one scripture she loved to repeat that I will never forget: "For the wages of sin is death; but the gift of God is eternal life through Jesus Christ our Lord." (Romans 6:23) KJV. I would literally go from drunk to frightened. Momma sowed the seeds that eventually drew me to the foot of the cross in repentance.

My dad, affectionately known as L.C., always had a pastoral anointing on his life and it led him directly into ministry. When a pastor is called, his whole family has a part to play in ministry as well. Like I said before, I was a Preacher's Kid! One of the hardest parts about being a PK growing up is that the expectations are set extremely high. I had to attend bible study, and go to prayer meetings throughout the week. On the weekends, there was Sunday school and Sunday church services. I even had to sing and lead songs in the choir and *I couldn't even sing*!

I had become so involved in ministry and I went to church so much that when I became an adult, I literally did not want to go to church at all! People have always stereotyped preacher's kids. They say that we are the worst ones! It's very tough maintaining an image when the image doesn't fit you. I was a tomboy still trying to figure out this thing called life. From my perspective, growing up as a preacher's kid made it extremely difficult to adjust and figure out who I really was without the eyes of the congregation leering, watching, dissecting, and judging my every move and decision.

Although I had some struggles being a preacher's kid, there were some awesome advantages. One of the most memorable ones is that I had the opportunity to be around some amazing leaders by default. Many of the church Elders, Missionaries, and Pastor's wives took up time with me and gave me something to aspire to. Although he does not pastor anymore, my dad has always been my spiritual guide and my favorite Elder until this day. I've watched him bring many souls to Christ. If God didn't give me the dad that He gave me (who stood in as my father and my spiritual covering), I don't know where I would be right now. His example has allowed me to be rooted and grounded in the word of God today.

As a young child in elementary school, I was curious about what it would be like to **not** be a preacher's kid. I started to hang with a group of people that did everything under the sun. That wasn't really who I was! My grades started dropping and I ended up being retained in the fifth grade. So many times, godly parents try to instill righteousness into their children to help them avoid the consequences they must face when they decide to stray away or allow people to steer them in a direction that is foreign to them. Today, I wish I would have taken advantage of their leadership in Christ. It was their prayers and supplication that were made on my behalf that helped draw me back to God and discover true freedom. After that walk of shame that occurred when I failed the fifth grade, I was ok with being a preacher's kid again! There's nothing like a good ole' *embarrassment* to help get you back on the right track.

By sixth grade, I had found something that I was really good at. Basketball became my life and the most exciting part of it! This game became the object of my affection and my true heart's desire! That's all I wanted to do. I wanted to explore different facets of the game of basketball the better I got at it, so I begged my parents to get me a basketball goal. I never in a million years thought that they would actually get it. They made me the happiest kid in the world the day I came home from school and saw that goal sitting up in our driveway. I honestly thought it was Christmas in July! I don't recall ever getting into trouble again during those younger years, because that BALL LIFE had my full attention.

Another grade level of people caught up with me when I retained. At one point, it felt like failing was one of the worst things that could have ever happened to me. It ended up not being *all bad* after all. During that year, I met my best friend Kutheria McKnight, who is still my best friend to this very day. Although I experienced a great deal of pain and shame in failing, it also gave me a friendship that brought me happiness and understanding… and it taught me a valuable lesson on being aware of the company that you keep.

The bible says "Don't be fooled by those who say such things, for bad company corrupts good character. Think carefully about what is right and stop sinning (1 Corinthians 15:33-34 NLT). Everyone that confesses to be your friend doesn't always hang out with you for the right reasons. Their motives can be deceiving and they can be used as tools in the devil's hand that help lead you to a life of rebellion.

One of the main points on the devil's agenda is to target you when you are a righteous seed and when God has His hands on you. I now realize that Satan targeted me to be a part of his plan from a young age. Nevertheless, I truly believe that God had His hands on me before I ever knew who He was, and that was what kept the enemy at bay. The Word of

God says in Isaiah 41:10 KJV: "Fear not, for I am with you; be not dismayed, for I am your God; I will strengthen you, I will help you, I will uphold (hold you up) you with my righteous right hand." Throughout the years, God's right hand holding me up had to be what kept me going.

"Before I formed you in the belly, I knew you, before you were born I set you apart; I appointed you as a prophet to the nations."
(Jeremiah 1:5 [NIV])

2
OUT-OF-BOUNDS

When a player steps on or across the boundary lines with their feet or touches any object that is out of play.

"**Man**"...I shouted and shook my head in frustration. I'm disgusted because It looks like my fade away didn't actually work for me this time. As Lisa Leslie blocked my shot and scored on the other end, the crowd went WILD! Rebecca Lobo got the ball and passed it back to me. I shot a three-pointer and the ball went through the hoop with the swish sound and next thing I know...my alarm clock starts going off?!?!?

Wake up Miriam!

Once I made the basketball team, I began to eat, drink, sleep and even DREAM basketball! The basketball goal my parents got me paid off a great deal! For me to say that I was elated during this time in my life would be an understatement. I began to feel so much more in tune with the world now that I discovered how the game of basketball had given my entire existence such a great sense of structure and responsibility. Now, I'm more than just a preacher's kid, and my teammates are counting on me to be my best self at all times! Only thing was: I started to realize that this was not just about the game of basketball itself, as the lessons and language of the game seemed to eventually shift into the layout for my entire life in so many different ways!

As I transitioned into middle school, I tried my best to excel in my studies and to stay focused. I used all of my free time after practice and school to polish up my athletic skills. I spent the first year on the junior varsity team with very limited play time (PT), as I was a new team member. I had become a solid honor roll student. The school year flew by, and although I'd started to get some PT, I hadn't become a starting player YET. Nevertheless, I was confident that this waiting period would soon be over, as I got better and better at basketball every day. However, I had come to a place where I started to feel impatient and frustrated about having so much time on the bench.

All of the time I spent benched found me outside of the playing boundaries. I grew weary very quickly of watching the excitement from the sidelines and not being a part of the action on the court! Sometimes, I felt like running on the court without being subbed in… which would cause me to be ejected from the game. I knew enough to know that I had to exercise restraint if I ever wanted a real opportunity to show my coach, my teammates, and everyone else in attendance that I had what it takes to help lead my team to victory. It was an amazing feat to be able to control myself in this manner and "wait my turn" until my coach gave me the green light to get in the game and begin to work my magic on the court. I later wondered why this kind of temperance didn't transfer off the court, because it seemed like my life would soon enough become wild and uncontrolled so rapidly that I didn't have the opportunity to pause long enough to see what was really going on.

As a growing teenager, I continued to evolve and go through changes physically, mentally, and emotionally. In fact, my emotions had become one of the most powerful measures of whether or not I was adhering to the set boundaries for my life, and they were even the deciding factor when it came to me needing to exert self-control. That has proven not to be the most reliable measuring system, as emotions are unpredictable. Like most girls my age, I had thoughts, imaginations, wishes, and hopes for a lover. My lover just happened to be brown with black stripes (yes, it was a basketball)!

Thankfully, the enemy held off a little while longer before he came for my life and my core desires...because I was still laser-focused and preoccupied with excelling in my favorite sport. I was still bound to the bench, but I was so eager and determined to get out on that basketball court! I began to challenge myself to push even harder in practice. I grew by leaps and bounds in my craft and became more strategic and forward-thinking regarding the overall game. Throughout another summer of practicing, tryouts, and then going back into our regular season practices, I had become a consistently great player all around. By the time the next season came along, I was starting my second year on the junior varsity basketball team. I had a vision for this athletic year, and I was armed with the fruits of my labor from practice and preparation. Hard work was better than talent to me because it always made me feel confident and unstoppable!

I was so excited, because I had finally made it to a space where I'd secured some real playing time on the court! I remember my first game. I was given jersey #45 to wear. At the time, I didn't care about what number I had on. I was far more interested in showing what

I'd been working so hard for. I had an amazing season! It was so great that after the season was over, I was promoted to the varsity team and I hadn't even made it to the ninth grade yet!

Some more time passed, and I was blessed and fortunate enough to make a name for myself here in my town and surrounding area(s) because of my basketball skills. I'd matriculated to high school at this point, and things were continuing to change all around me. I'd just watched my favorite player graduate (a local great named Michellda Bradshaw) and all I could think about was getting her jersey number #30 and living up to her talents to make her proud. That year, I asked my coach if I could be the new #30 for the JFK Hornets. She said yes- and when she gave me jersey #30, I was so honored to have it and I wore it with great pride!

Game after game, I continuously grew into greatness whenever I was inside the paint! Like Michellda, I was placed in the position of a power forward on my team. It was my goal to be the best power forward in the district.

Gradually, I was able to shift into any position I was put into and give a peak performance because my thoughts connected with my actions so quickly out on the court. I was truly thankful even at that stage of my life that the hard work that I had put into my dreams had now manifested into success on the court, and that brought me so much joy!

As a skilled player, I had several signature plays, but THE CROSSOVER was one of my most masterful moves against my opponents. I became known for faking out other players while rapidly switching the ball from one hand to the other and changing directions! I was a beast because I had a knack for attacking my defense by starting off calmly, then becoming aggressive in an instant to drive the ball forward and score, throwing my opponents off. Another way I would attack the defense is to examine their body position and use what I saw as leverage to fake my opponents out. I'd go to the left, make my opponent drop her lead foot, step over to the right…then step back to create space to beat my defender and score a winning shot for my team! While I was so busy crossing over in basketball, the enemy was setting up an ungodly crossover of his own in my life in order to begin to **harden** my heart.

I remember going to study hall for one hour daily for an entire semester. All I ever did while I was there was think about basketball and what my next game would be like for the team and I. One day, a distraction came knocking at my door. I would see this guy, a senior, first glancing, then staring at me continuously from a distance. He would proceed with the same routine everyday that I saw him. It didn't dawn on me at the beginning that he was trying to get my attention, because I knew nothing much about guys at the time. I slowly began to grasp the concept that he was trying to draw me to him with his constant stare.

Maintaining my focus in basketball meant everything to me, and I never thought in a million years that something or someone could get into my mental space. At that time, it was my school work and basketball only that held my attention. I was only in ninth grade and I didn't yet have the wisdom to understand how to eliminate distractions from my life. Besides, this was something new for me. I never lost focus on the game of basketball, but I did gain a *new* focus in wanting to know more about boys. How do you converse with a boy? What should you even say to a boy? How do you kiss a boy?

This newfound attention had my mind racing. I quickly became sexually inquisitive. Curiosity in all forms started to manifest deeply in my mind. After a time of staring, this guy started speaking to me. Speaking to me transitioned into walking me home from school. This started a pattern for us. I found him very attractive. I started enjoying the conversations and reminiscing on the walks even after I made it home.

One day after basketball practice, I went home and a girl from school called me with him on the other end of the phone on three-way. I thought it was a bit strange that he was on the other end. She started talking and said: "Hey Miriam! My friend likes <u>Spalding</u> as well and he likes her too, but she told him that he had to make a choice between you and her." She continued, "So Spalding, who's it going to be?" Spalding then proceeded with the words *"I choose her"* (the other girl). After I heard his words, there was a moment of silent contemplation that hit me. Immediately after that, shortness of breath hit me, alongside a wave of pain and sadness that I had not experienced before. I didn't know what was happening to me, so I hung up the phone as I simultaneously spit out the words "Okay that's fine."

As odd as this may sound to some, I never knew anything about feelings until that moment. I discovered then what feelings felt like for the first time, and I had such a rude introduction to the whole concept! I decided that day that I literally *never* wanted to feel or have feelings again. Even though my heart was experiencing something new and painful, I gave my mind complete access to the state of being rejected. I felt naked and alone. I couldn't shake the feeling of being unwanted and having self-doubt. While I was winning in basketball, the game of self-degradation had won prime real estate in my heart and mind.

It was so hard to get my focus back and try hard not to be curious about boys. Spalding was gone. In that season, he no longer existed to me-even though he was still somewhere around. Rejection put me in a place that I had never been before, and a place that I didn't even know existed. This event triggered me in a way that put me on a road to becoming emotionally numb in some very profound ways. So in the unsettling mixture of curiosity and pain, I made a life-changing decision to make myself physically available to guys. It was a conscious choice that I made to cover up and protect myself from what I didn't know at the time was the sting of rejection. I wanted to feel wanted with no feelings and no strings attached. I gave THEM permission to cross the boundary of no return with me without any resistance. I was always in control but **never** in charge. For the first time in my life, I had given myself away to people instead of God, and that's the moment when I lost control and began life out-of-bounds.

I allowed rejection to cause a great deal of destruction in my life. I was taken deeper and deeper into sin. I went so deep so quickly that I didn't recognize the trap of the devil that was waiting to consume me. I couldn't break free from the manifestations of rejection. I had become so addicted to so many sinful things that I fouled out (reached my limit) of the game with guys- almost losing count of the bodies that I crossed. I had gotten so far gone that I got to a place where I couldn't hear from God anymore, and I became unrecognizable to even myself. I didn't realize how much being rejected would affect every aspect of my life.

Jesus defeated sin and death because of the Father's love. We can be set free by that same love. The Bible says that God's love heals a spirit of rejection because "perfect love casts out fear" (1 John 4:18). One of the things that the Spirit of Rejection is filled with is the Spirit of Fear. For some, it manifests as a fear of being alone. For others, it manifests as a fear of being unwanted and unloved. For many, it can manifest as a fear of the unknown, which can keep us stuck and unable to move into our assignment and the destiny that God has designed for our lives. Rejection can set up a stronghold, but God's love will always be stronger.

*For God has not given us the spirit of fear, but of **power** and of **love** and of a **sound mind**. (2 Timothy 1:7 [NKJV])*

3
FAST BREAK

A quick offensive drive toward a goal in an attempt to score before the opponent's defense is set up.

After the Spirit of Rejection caused a breach in my heart, the enemy came hard and fast! I must say, a fast break can truly keep you on your toes because your opponent never gives you a chance to slow down enough to catch your breath. I transitioned quickly on the basketball team and now I'm a starter. While I was breaking fast on the court, the enemy was once again making a fast break move right back on me! Every chance the enemy got to try to make me force the ball the other way, I was always unprepared to stop him! The enemy had become a rival that I didn't have the knowledge or skill set to defeat. When rejection hit my life, I missed my shot and Satan took advantage of my mistakes. Now, every turnover and error of judgment in my life has become the most difficult task to overcome.

As I attempted to move forward from that place of rejection, I was determined deep down inside that I would build an impenetrable wall within my heart so that I would never have to experience that type of hurt again. I never understood how something that seemed so small as someone choosing someone else over me could cause my heart to be on such an emotional rollercoaster. I went into protective mode so hard that even the faint *smell* of feelings made me shut down like an old, broken 1971 Ford Pinto. At this point, both my heart and my body now have a substantial deficiency. Like that old Pinto, my heart could now be qualified as a "lemon." I couldn't get a replacement for my heart and I couldn't get a refund for my body, so I decided that sex would become my brand new hobby and my chosen bad habit all at the same time.

Although I picked up a newfound interest in sexual activity, I still never found the opportunity to make peace with being rejected. It made me feel indifferent toward the idea of being in a relationship. It crushed my confidence and had me continuously questioning what was wrong with me. To me, the idea of being turned down by someone who chose someone else over you hurts much worse than someone who just rejects you without comparing you to or making a valuation of you against another person. I was physically tormented and emotionally damaged. My emphasis on rejection at this point may sound like a dead horse that I'm beating, but it truly changed me at the most foundational level. Rejection even altered how I thought about who I really was and how I saw and perceived myself. As bad as those feelings hurt me, I had no idea that I would soon collide with pain and hurt far greater than the one that the nasty stain of rejection had left on my life.

I wish somehow I could have been prepared for the knock on my door that would alter my whole entire existence. Now, that day started as normal as it always did, with my siblings and I heading to school and my parents heading to work. After a full day of school and basketball practice, I was extremely exhausted. Every single day right after practice, I went home to take a nap. It was the third day of the month in January of the year 2000, and my dad woke me up out of my sleep with a cracking tone in his voice…I heard him say "Let's go." There was something in his demeanor that jolted me out of my nap. I jumped up and started putting on my clothes, only to be given the most devastating news anyone could ever receive. I felt like I was in a dream sequence as I heard my dad continue to say, "Your grandparents were involved in a car accident that took both of their lives!" Suddenly, severe chest pains hit me like a ton of bricks. They kicked in hard and fast...followed by the weakening of my legs, an irregular heartbeat, and a shortness of breath that had now become familiar to me. Now that I think of it, those first moments where I felt the sting of the death of my grandparents laid the foundation for some of the anxiety issues I've had to face throughout my life's journey.

After rushing to the scene of the accident with my dad, I jumped out of the car and started running. I was stopped by police officers who wouldn't allow me to go any further. I lifted up my head and I saw my grandparents' car from afar and I knew immediately that the collision was fatal. I stood in the middle of the highway weeping profusely with disbelief as the waves of sadness and the coldness of abandonment and loneliness slowly began to attack my heart. I was so full of anger and resentment. I was mad at my grandparents for leaving me and I was mad at God for taking them away. Traffic was so backed up to the point where all of the lights in the distance made the small town of Merigold, Mississippi glow like a big city.

The police instructed us to go to the hospital immediately. Once we made it to the hospital, the waiting room was filled with Billy's family members. "Billy" was the name that I eventually found out went with the person that the newspapers later identified to be the driver of the car that collided head-on with my grandparents. I was so confused at the time because I thought that he had passed away as well. His family was screaming and crying a river! As I proceeded past the waiting room, those double doors opened and there was Billy, ALIVE and WELL and waiting to see a doctor because he hurt his *leg*. I began to pace the floor anxiously...full of anger and rage...wanting to kill everything and everyone that was connected to Billy!

At that moment, I truly didn't understand any of what was going on. I would have never thought that godly people could die this way. I thought God was their protector. I remember thinking a series of thoughts and feeling a range of emotions that brought up questions like, "God, I thought you were my protector too? How could you let this happen to them?

This is wrong on so many levels!!! God, why aren't you answering me?" I started screaming to the top of my lungs, and in an outpour of tears and anger, I cried "Haven't I served you BEFORE God? God, why did Billy have to live?!?"

Days passed and I stayed at home from school for an entire week up until my grandparents' double funeral. I didn't go home. I stayed at my grandparents' home in my grandfather's room. I wished to hear his voice one last time. On the day of the funeral, my heart was beating so fast and loud that I could hear it in my ears. As I proceeded through the church doors with my family, I thought I was going to lose my mind seeing both of my grandparents in a casket. My legs began to shake and weaken the closer I got to their bodies. I tried to hold back the tears, but the hurt and pain wouldn't allow me to. Before I knew it, I had broken down in tears, devastation and anguish. After walking back and forth to their caskets, I stood there in disbelief. I felt lost trying to figure out how God let something so horrible happen to such amazing people and why He allowed them to leave the earth in such a tragic manner. I mean, not only did they simply pass away, but the seat belt broke my grandmother's neck and the motor crushed my grandfather's chest! Whenever this horrifying truth played back in my mind, I would have frequent episodes of rage, weeping, and despair. I was so sick that it honestly felt like the end of the world.

Needless to say, this fast-break move was the enemy's play of the year! The devil went for my lifeline, and it literally felt like he knocked the wind out of me! It seemed to me that he had already won whatever game he was playing, because he definitely was not playing fair. Where was the referee? Everything began to feel unbearable, especially now that the team captains (my grandparents) have been taken out of the game. How could I ever even win such a complex sport as life without them? Losing my grandparents would prove to be one of the most significant devastations of my life to-date. Only God would be able to help me put the pieces of my life back together again.

For His anger is but for a moment, His favor is for life; Weeping may endure for a night, But joy comes in the morning. (Psalms 30:5 [NKJV])

TIME-OUT

LET'S PRAY

Lord God, here I am standing in the need of prayer. I haven't always been faithful to you, but you still chose to give me life and allowed me to be here. Thank you for not giving up on me. Lord, forgive me for everything that I've done that doesn't line up with your Word. I surrender my all to you God. Lord, please give me a heart like yours so I can be more like you. Let your will be done and your glory be revealed in Jesus's Name.

Father, I release the spirit of rejection into Your hands. I give You my thoughts, my desires, and everything else that is not pleasing to You. Help me to walk in love and not let the spirit of rejection destroy my future. With Your help, I surrender my anger to You and I give You my resentment as well. Lord, open my eargates so that I can begin to hear You clearly concerning my heart's posture. Lead me to a place of righteousness and please don't let the spirit of rejection cause me to be hurt or hurt others.

I bind the spirit of lust that seeks to destroy my body and my mind. Although my flesh is weak and I want to do certain things...help me to put it down Lord, so that You can pick me up. Take away the feelings of loneliness, brokenness, and the emptiness that is rooted in my lust. Help me to set boundaries for myself so that I can overcome lust.

I bind the spirit of sexual immorality. I give you every unfaithful thought that lingers in my mind. Help me to flee and be completely free from sexual immorality. Lord, give me the wisdom and understanding to know that my body is the temple of the Holy Ghost. God, this battle is yours and I repent. I willingly walk away from every sin and temptation that seeks to destroy my own body in Jesus's name. Amen.

Part Two

SECOND QUARTER

THE SHOT OF SHAME

"Just when you think you're covered, shame will pull the covers off!"

~Miriam Tamar Holmes

4
AIR BALL

To completely miss the rim and backboard with a shot.

The worst thing in the world to do in a basketball game is to shoot an air ball. The embarrassment does not go away until you redeem yourself and score. I always pictured myself hitting "nothing but net" when I'm in go-mode, finessing my way down the court. So whenever I threw an airball, I just **had** to try again. When I reached the point where every move I made had my life looking like one giant "air ball", I knew deep down inside that these were not the plays that I wanted to define me. In the name of trying to recover from missing those game-winning shots, I started making erratic plays and even what could be described as some fatal errors on life's court. These plays not only jeopardized the game, but had me in danger of being benched, ejected, and looking sadly from the sidelines! I became so disillusioned during this season that I started throwing shots in the wrong basket and scoring points for the other team!

Satan had gotten the advantage over me, because I wasn't just missing the rim in the game, I was also missing what was going on in the realm of the spirit. My eyes were closed to this unseen realm, and that caused me to be double-minded and unstable in all of my ways. Instead of seeking God's help, I had now chosen to fight life's battles alone. This was one of the biggest mistakes of my life!

Normally when shooting an air ball, one is exposed to a great deal of shame. I wanted to escape from the pain of failure and distance myself from the person that I had become. Just as Adam and Eve bit into the forbidden fruit in the Garden of Eden, realized they were naked and hid themselves (Genesis 3:7-11)...the very same sins of desire and indulgence led me into hiding as well. I hid from God and His presence because I was weak and wanton, living in a world of sin and wallowing in the forbidden. I was in desperate need of redemption. I was literally "out there"- open and exposed not only to God, but now the entire crowd knew what I'd done because they had front-row seats to watch **<u>all</u>** of the action.

After numerous turnovers, the enemy had now scored on me so many times that I didn't have the practical discernment to seek out the wisdom for proper godly living. I was so ashamed that I had even begun to hide from my true self. I continued to remain a counterfeit to the church congregation, and I still kept up a false appearance with my parents as well. It had become a bit exhausting to try to continue being that pseudo-religious young woman that my parents wanted me to be, as it was not authentic to the person I was actually becoming. The ugly truth is that, although I was still trying to maintain the image of who they thought I was, those unacknowledged feelings inside of me had increasingly gotten to a point where I didn't want to pretend anymore. Yes I did feel guilty for the things I'd been doing, but I didn't have the strength to withstand temptation.

Although basketball was still my first love at this point, I had a new and growing interest in the pleasures that sex opened me up to now enjoy and experience. I had experienced the ecstasy that sexual chemistry had introduced me to, and chasing that feeling quickly became my new main focus. After the hurt that rejection made me feel, I began to use sex as a means of protecting myself from ever having to feel that same level of pain again. This began to fortify and strengthen the wall that had erected itself within my heart and desensitized me in so many ways emotionally. I could now be intimate **without** involving my heart strings.

My heart for people in general never changed because of how I was raised, but the fact that I was becoming a puppet in the devil's hands hardened me to a point that fulfilling my selfish desires was my main priority. I'd developed a habit of making poor decisions, which led me to a series of continuous bad habits. Those once uninvited thoughts and desires had now become my daily meditation. There weren't too many things that I didn't want to do, and I didn't employ limits on the activities that I began to indulge in. I couldn't believe how I had reached a point in my life where I desired other things more than I desired God!

Sadly, I was so caught up in the sinful pleasures of the world that I no longer gave God the worship and love that He so rightfully deserves. My body was still present at church, but my mind and heart were completely absent. Oddly enough, I was on the threshold of still wanting to submit to God, but as I fell deeper and deeper into sin, I literally became LOST. God is a jealous God. The bible says "their loyalty is divided between God and the world, and they are unstable in everything they do " (James 1:8 NLT). I became the poster child for a double-minded human being.

I rapidly crossed over from one bad habit to the next. I was moving through this world, carrying the weight of a compulsive sexual addiction alongside a weakness for alcohol. I reached a juncture where this behavior became too difficult for me to control. Being intoxicated and being sexually active were the only plays that I wanted to make at this time, because I couldn't bear to continue feeling the harshness of the reality that death dropped off at my doorstep the day that I lost my grandparents. I desperately wanted to be NUMB. I had become addicted to the comforts that soothed my body and numbed my mind to help me cover up the pain. I had even stopped at one point to ask myself "Who am I?" I had become utterly blinded, with closed ears and a darkened mindset. It felt like I was in a desert all alone with no cell phone reception. I couldn't call on Jesus even if I wanted to. My signal had become far too weak!!!

Many people don't think that the unseen realm of the spirit is as real as the material world that they can see. Not only is it real, it's more real than most people could ever imagine. Out of the blue, I started to hear the curiosity of people buzzing around me with the question "Are you gay?" Sure, I was a tomboy...but the thought of being gay had never once crossed my mind up to this point. It's so crazy how the words and opinions of others can get into your own thought patterns when they are continuously spoken....and how, if you are not careful, you may begin to actually manifest the words that are spoken in your hearing! That proves that words can not only hurt, but that they can affect your life in such a powerful way if you are not watchful and intentional. Our tongues have a lot of power, so you have to be very careful of the things that you say to people. The word of God says, "The tongue can bring death or life; those who love to talk will reap the consequences" Proverbs 18:21 (NLT).

The constant implications regarding my sexuality continued! Those suggestions began to produce something on the inside of me that left me in an overwhelmingly dark and fearful place. At this juncture, the internal battle of spiritual warfare concerning my identity is a voice playing at maximum volume within my mind and in my heart. Not only are people questioning my identity, but I began to question myself and everything that I've known up to this point in my life. The enemy didn't want to come in as a **normal** guest through the front door, but being the evil and uncircumcised Philistine that he is, he wanted to creep in through the back door in silence. Before this, I thought that I was doing sin at its highest level and boy was I wrong! Satan had conjured up a plan to plant a new identity inside of me that I was totally unaware of and could have never imagined for myself in even my wildest imagination! It turned out to be the lid on [1]Pandora's Box that would open up a whole new reality in my life and in my story.

They are headed for destruction. Their God is their appetite, they brag about shameful things, and they think only about this life here on earth.

(Philippians 3:19 [NLT])

---

1. *Pandora's Box* is a prolific source of troubles. In Greek mythology, Pandora was endowed with every grace. Out of curiosity, she opened a box and released all the evils that might plague humankind.

5
BLOCK OUT

When a defensive player blocks the offensive player's path to the basket when a shot goes up.

I'm in my senior year of high school now, and I have chosen to continue doing immoral things to keep my mind and my heart at bay. This has been an unwinnable war. I kept feeling like I would be able to block out this rebellious world that I'd been living in and open myself to God...if I could just pull myself onto the "side of the road" and find a quiet place to pray. The only problem with this theory was the fact that it is so extremely difficult to see in the dark! The pathway to God hadn't been visible to me for a while at that point. I'd been living blindly... and that fortifies such a strong sense of darkness internally, which eventually darkens everything around you. For some time now, things had really progressed in my life, and I was feeling like I was almost out of money from paying the wages of sin out-of-pocket because this was the course that I had chosen to follow.

Thankfully, I was unable to fulfill every one of my hearts' desires at this point, because I was still living in my parents' home and under their authority. Church attendance was NOT AN OPTION with my parents, so I was still getting up on Sundays for Sunday school and morning worship service, and still going to Bible study during the week. On the other hand, I was being sneaky-bending and breaking the rules whenever and wherever I could do so undetected. Still a basketball fanatic, I did whatever was necessary to qualify to continue to play the game I loved so much!

Balling was a priority for me, and as an athlete, I cared about my body and being in shape enough to give an optimal performance on the court. Basketball was not just my passion, but it also ended up being a type of "saving grace" in my life during these defining moments.

One day, I overheard one of the cheerleaders at one of our home games call me GAY. Just hearing that word upset me, so I felt the words "bet" come up in my heart alongside this challenge to my femininity! A feeling of revenge led me to be like "since you think I'm gay, imma show you how gay I'm NOT." Vengefully, I decided at that very moment that I would sleep with her boyfriend....not once but continuously. Without much attention to consequence, I moved even further from home base and continued operating from a place of recklessly fulfilling whatever the occasion, the person or my body called for on any given day.

I was in a place and space where sex and the feelings that it gave me had become an **end**, and the guys that I slept with were simply a tool, or a *means* to an end. I wasn't looking for a boyfriend or a relationship at that moment any more than I was already married to the game of basketball- and it alone was the object of my true affection. It was just that I had literally found my escape from the after-effects of rejection in a **_feeling_**. When I opened up my legs, I closed my heart and the feelings that came afterwards became sufficient within themselves. Mix that with a little alcohol, and now I'm on cloud nine, living the lifestyle that's not abnormal for many teens that you know, love, and parent today.

In all of this, I was still a baller who loved ballin' so much that I not only played with my high school team, but I would also go to the catholic school after the school day ended (and on the weekends) to play *even more* basketball. We called this spot "The Cap". There was a college girl who would be there playing on the court as well. Let's call her "Ms. Broom." Ms. Broom was cool and she was a baller too, with many skills on the basketball court. We would play and she would engage me, not just on the court, but also in a friendly manner outside of the court. She was what I eventually came to know as a "stud", a girl who looked like she was "gay" or presented herself in a masculine manner. At that time, I hadn't yet discovered what being gay fully even meant!

After so long, Ms. Broom made it clear that she liked me. I was confusingly curious as to why and what that meant for me on my end. One day after practice, Ms. Broom took me home and we ended up kissing on the way. Although I felt a rush in my hormones and everything inside of me rose up, I still felt weird. It didn't seem "special" to me at the time- it just happened to be my first time kissing a girl. I was a nervous wreck because I thought everyone would automatically know what happened, and I was worried about what everyone would think. I kinda felt sick because it didn't feel like that was who I was. I was perplexed at my **own** self, puzzled and trying to understand why I chose to do this... and what this now meant for me.

Life continued, and Ms. Broom and I went through my senior year of high school exploring. The kissing and touching she and I engaged in may not have necessarily qualified as a full-blown homosexual experience to some (I definitely didn't think of it as one for some reason), but it pre-set the stage that soon opened a door to the world of homosexuality and the idea of living an alternative lifestyle. Making out with Ms. Broom soon taught me that the feelings were more heightened engaging with women (even in a brief capacity) than it was dealing and being with men. After that first kiss with her, I was certain that everything "felt better" as we explored together in a way that was familiar and it seemed that I was naturally understood. I didn't know why at the time, but I had already learned one of the fundamental "truths" that keep people locked into same-sex relationships…and that surrounds the premise that the physical pleasures even in simply making out feel a thousand times more magnified and stronger at **her** touch compared to all the times that I had been touched and had sex with any one of the guys that I had encountered up to this point. The heightened sensitivity is familiar because there is a FAMILIAR

SPIRIT at the root of it, controlling even the physical sensations...another trick of the enemy...but that is key information that I will speak about briefly in Chapter 12.

After a while, this new thing that crept quietly and unassumingly into my life along with Ms. Broom felt so wrong overall, that it literally scared me straight! All this church girl had ever been taught fundamentally was the biblical story of Adam and Eve. My parents knew God's Word and had instructed me well. I had no reason not to accept the scriptures in the book of Genesis as truth or question this story regarding the origin of mankind, and I was not about to start now! Even in the midst of my sin, I was still trying to make my way back to the norm-which was all that I'd ever known!

I remember going to the bowling alley for a night of fun. In passing, I saw this guy looking at me. Let's call him " Mr. Letterman." So I waved at Mr. Letterman, smiled and said "Hi!" Mr. Letterman responded back with a smile on his own and said, "Who me?" I replied "Yes, you" and we shared a hearty laugh together. He had the most beautiful smile I'd ever seen in the world! He came into my life at the perfect time, because he saw a beauty in me that I couldn't possibly see in myself right then. He was different from any other guy that I had come across! He always followed up on his claims of wanting to spend time with me with both effort and action. He was my "Mr. Right," so I invited him home to meet my parents. I remember him being so respectful that night and I couldn't wait to see him again. The next time we met, I couldn't keep my hands off him! Honestly, I wanted to take things all the way, but I decided against it. I had so much respect for him because our encounters were so meaningful.

I enjoyed every moment that I spent with Mr. Letterman. We never argued and we never fought. Every moment was full of joy and even started to feel like love for me! Little did I know that unfortunately, Mr. Letterman's goodness wouldn't be enough to keep me on the well-traveled road that we were on, because there was a fork in that road shortly up ahead. I was already emotionally damaged.

We grew apart and went our separate ways. Years later, we met up again. By that time, the enemy had already completed a full block-out within my identity! I still cared for him a great deal...to the point where I had to walk away from him completely, not because of him but because of me and who I had become. I was now a "sexual being" and that part of me was driving my life forward! The space that he'd found me in during that season made it inevitable that we'd connect physically, after all we'd shared in the past emotionally. The sexual feeling had become so strong over me that it was like crack and I kept going back! This sexual stronghold had full control of me and it was now DEFINITELY in charge and calling ALL the shots!

Most women are more emotional than men. I now know that the levels of emotional vulnerability and openness that flow almost effortlessly from a woman are naturally more familiar to another woman, so the intimacy and closeness that occurs when women bond and discuss issues and feelings will transfer into sex if a physical line is crossed.

That goes a lot further than any guy just getting you alone and getting down to business, and that's what many men do and how they typically move in casual, not-committal sex. I knew this all too well, because I was fully engaged and sexually active with guys and yet there was still this gentleness coming from this female that kept me wondering and excited. Yes, I found myself exploring again after that first encounter with Ms. Broom and even enjoying myself. Ironically, I was double-minded…as I still managed to have an issue with this newfound focus on my sexuality that people were starting to give me.

As good as I felt in sin, there was still some THINGS in me that I could not deny-and that was the PULL of God's plan and purpose for my life, the prayers that had been and were being prayed on my behalf, and the fact that I felt that God had something different for me than all I was currently into. God was actively trying to get my attention, and I both noticed and felt it. I was definitely operating recklessly, but my conscience was not gone. I cannot say that righteousness was even on the forefront of my mind, but there was a disturbance in my soul. This lack of comfort in sin is what activated the Spirit of Conviction that began to rest on my life heavily later on in my journey.

Looking back on life as a senior in high school, I was an honor roll student, my basketball season was amazing (we were district champs that advanced to the state), and my parents were pretty much proud of me. If you look at our world today, you could describe me as your typical teenager. Although the loss of my grandparents was still near and dear to my heart, I was able to move forward, make new friends and enjoy my life up to this point. I was a church-going girl and by any "normal" standards, I was a good, decent, and respectful kid. Even to myself, it appeared that my issues with rejection were now <u>seemingly</u> a thing of the past. I was sexually active and all of that action kinda kept the misery at bay, at least in that season.

I made it clear at the beginning of this book that I was just a tomboy. At that time, I was into something new and although I liked it, I was not gay. I stood up tall like Shaq under that basketball rim of my life BLOCKING OUT everyone and everything that tried to suggest otherwise or define me in a way that I wasn't clear about myself. I was in a place where I thought I was in control of my life, but the fact of the matter was that I was actually OUT of control. I was fighting all I could not to be what the world had suddenly kept trying to define and name me, but I did not have the help or the practical resources to fight and win a battle that was so much bigger than me at the time.

My parents were praying, and I know that their prayers shielded me from dangers seen and unseen. Although this is what kept me through it all, I wonder what would have happened if there was a saved and relatable youth leader at my church at the time, truly steering me in the right and godly direction. What if there was another saved teenager in my class that I could have been myself with and someone that I could have shared my questions and challenges with? That's why I want to take a pause here and note the importance of how the life that we live and the choices that we make are not just for us.

Oftentimes, we stay in sin, taking advantage of God's grace over our lives and reject His timing, trying to fulfill our own lusts. Meanwhile, there's someone's life that we may be anointed to directly impact and help. God could be calling us to bring His healing power through His Word to them in a way that could alter their direction, perception, and their course, and even protect them from the evil of this world. Stop here and ask yourself this question: Is my lack of submission to God and His plan for my life holding up someone else's deliverance? Those who know and sense God's calling to change and help others change as well cannot afford to lag leisurely or wallow in sin. There's often a price to pay (think: someone else's blood on your hands) since everyone won't necessarily have as many opportunities to get it right as we may have been graced and blessed with, and they may be literally counting on us to be the HERO in their story!

I can honestly say at this point of my journey, I needed a hero to step in and help me before the floodgates of hell opened up over my life. I got in the driver's seat of the car that contained my destiny and as you will read in the upcoming chapters of this book, I drove speedily into oncoming traffic, almost forfeiting my future, my purpose, and God's plans for my life and even for the lives of my children and grandchildren! God has more for you just like He had so much more in store for me, and I hope you can feel my sentiment so much that you are inspired to do something different today.

Have you been sensing that you need to go ahead and make some real changes in your life and in your lifestyle? Have you been feeling like you want to go to church and give your life over to God? Why wait? Stop right now and ask God to come into your heart and change you forever. Let Him know that you have faith in Him and believe that He died on the cross for your sins, and that He rose on the third day for your freedom. Go ahead right here, right now and surrender your all to God!

That if you confess with your mouth the Lord Jesus and believe in your heart that God has raised Him from the dead, you will be saved. For with the heart one believes unto righteousness, and with the mouth confession is made unto salvation. (Romans 10:9-10 [NKJV])

6

REBOUND

To gain possession of a missed shot after it bounces off the backboard or basket rim.

When you're rebounding in basketball, you have to be in the right position at all times. If you don't strategically set your stance, it's virtually impossible to win. I was on point in most games and I possessed the skill set to secure the rebound, but I didn't always use what I knew to make that play a successful one. Why? The truth is, running the court in a lengthy basketball game could become very exhausting, especially when you're a starter and you rarely ever get subbed out of the game. Regardless of this fact, I knew that if we were going to win, I had to muster up the strength to give it my all. So I focused in, put my eyes on the rim while simultaneously reaching around my back to feel for a body (keeping the opponent from getting in front of me), bent my knees, and then I lifted my hands to catch the ball in order to get the rebound. Now, I have a chance to bounce back, recover, and get things right. A second chance can make all the difference in the world.

Securing this particular rebound was pivotal, because this was the first game on a new court with a new team named "My Life, My Future." I'm staring in the face of a fresh start and new opportunities now that I'm a college student. Although my HBCU was only 45 miles from home, going away to college was my way of recovering and getting a second chance. College was the most natural transition for me at that time, and it was the perfect way to "rebound" my way out of regret and bad decisions. A rebound is a response to a missed shot and my missed shot in life was my past mistakes and my losses. My response to the rejection and pain that I had experienced in my life up to this point led me down a path of drinking, promiscuity and even an experience that I couldn't yet fully define. I had experienced so much in just a few short years, but I was certain that graduating high school would open me up to some new experiences that would make my life better. I expected that becoming a "college girl" would not only clear up some of my past mistakes, but somehow, it would help me want more out of life and automatically "fix" a lot of the things that had somehow managed to break in the last few years. Sadly, I wasn't the least bit aware of how my life was taking such a profound turn in a direction that I'd never in a million years imagined it would. My life didn't look like mine anymore. Ironically, I still had high hopes that my college experience would one day help me to become a better me.

As I expressed before, I was a college freshman and I was excited about the prospect of things looking up again in my life. I was the second one of my parent's children to leave home and become college-educated. I was finally FREE! I was excited about getting a chance to simply "do me" without the restrictions and rules that governed my parents' home. I was anxious to meet new people and see what this new season had to offer me.

I remember my first day moving into my college dorm room. I had my eyes on so many things and so many people. I was so ready to explore the feeling of being free. I didn't have to pretend anymore, and I could try whatever I was grown enough to try. It didn't take long for me to start trying things either.

I spoke about being scared straight in chapter 5 after my dealings with Ms. Broom. The confusion of that moment may have shocked me into disconnection, but the memory of the strong sensations my body felt still sat within me and *still* felt amazing! The truth of the matter is...that encounter was so new and different for me that I was fighting two ways: 1) not to be labeled as "gay" and 2) not to really give in to what I felt. I was so nervous about it that I tried to push it all to the back of my mind. Fast forward a year later, and I cannot shake the thoughts that Ms. Broom introduced me to and left me with.

The thing about sin is, it never gives you a heads up. If you don't kill it, it will pop back up and show out on you at the worst times possible. Although I was looking for change in the newness of my college experience, I was still the same old me, with all my bad habits and wayward thoughts. As a matter of a fact, my thought life pertaining to that encounter began to grow and take shape on its own. Out of the blue, I began to have daydreams about being intimate with the same sex. I became so inquisitive and interested in knowing more about what sex with a woman actually felt like. My daydreams and desires persisted until they went to their highest level. The curiosity had my mind in complete active mode...open to the opportunity that was just right around the corner and waiting for me to arrive on campus.

I'd only been in college for a week, yet I had already met someone that we will call

"Queen." Queen and I had quite a few things in common, and basketball was one of them. She was very good at playing my favorite game, and she was one of the star players on our girl's college team. I met Queen playing pickup games at the gym one evening. All of a sudden, there was a boldness that rose up in me that I never thought I had, and I approached her and gave her my phone number.

Although I was new to this lifestyle, somehow I just knew that I was ready for a new level in it and I wanted to go all the way with Queen and I did. It was my very first time! I felt so lost because I didn't know what I was doing but then I had a moment in my life that I will never forget. I had a change in my body that I had never experienced before. First, my heart rate began to increase rapidly, followed by shivers going down my spine, my entire body shaking with tremors and all of this ended with a scream so loud that it almost didn't even sound like my voice! I thought that I had just received a glimpse of heaven. It hit me like a ton of bricks moments later that I had just experienced my first orgasm with a woman. In both my mind and body, and to my complete satisfaction, I had completely crossed over to the other side.

This same-sex lifestyle became a stronghold that I couldn't pull down even if I wanted to. The power of lust working with my imagination was so strong on me because I gave in to so many lustful thoughts and desires. All this time, it never really dawned on me that I had gotten so far away from God. Everything that I was taught spiritually felt like it was all in vain. When you and God become distant, it's almost impossible to withstand temptation. I was already wrestling with a sexual stronghold overall, but now I've dived off into a deeper pit with same-sex interaction. I had full knowledge that what I was doing was wrong, but the struggle became so very real. The more that I thought about what Queen and I had just done, the stronger the desires grew. Now, it wasn't that I didn't want to seek God, but I was just too embarrassed to go to Him, still having lust in my eyes for a woman. I acted like I wasn't taught anything about

God. I never understood how I could be beyond shameful in my heart and mind towards God, yet...I could still hold these most beautiful and amazing flashbacks at the mere **thought** of the smell and touch of a woman. I quickly went from tomboy to masculine in no time. I went from wearing baggy women's clothing to wearing and sagging men's clothing. I even changed my underwear from panties to men's boxers. I was so afraid at the beginning of the manifestations that I let it consume my mind. Soon, it became who I was without a second thought.

It's so easy to lose control of yourself when you're living in sin. I had set goals for my success and even had a vision of myself coming out of the hole that I dug for myself shortly before I graduated high school. I wanted to change, but thoughts of change were quickly overshadowed by the desires that had taken over. Things began to shift quickly. It started with me not getting the basketball scholarship that I wanted. I was disappointed because I always saw myself playing professional basketball. It wasn't a day that went by that I didn't dream of it. So, it was a natural assumption that I would play college ball first. Ironically, it didn't take long at all for me to be okay with not getting the scholarship. I hadn't lost interest in the game of basketball at all, but I had lost interest in ME actively playing on a structured, strict, and regimented team. I was good although everything didn't "line up" because I was away from home and now, I had the freedom to explore everything that this new lifestyle had to offer. I was ready, and it was time for me to "LIVE IN MY TRUTH!"

But each man is tempted, when he is drawn away by his own lust, and enticed. Then when lust hath conceived, it bringeth forth sin: and sin, when it is finished, bringeth forth death.
(James 1:14-16 [KJV])

HALFTIME
GETTING TO KNOW MIRIAM

1. Favorite Movie: **The Proposal**

2. Dream Vacation: **Paris**

3. Favorite Food: **Fried chicken**

4. Strongest Spiritual Gift: **Discernment**

5. A challenge you have overcome recently: **The opinions of other people.**

6. Favorite Color: **Black**

7. Favorite physical trait about yourself: **My hair and my eyebrows**

8. A person you would like to meet: **Sarah Jakes**

9. What is something that always makes you smile? **Children in worship**

10. Favorite hobby? **Shooting pool**

11. My favorite way to spend down time: **Watching Movies**

12. Something that people would be surprised to know about me: **That I OVER-LOVE watching General Hospital**

13. **Who makes you laugh? DC Young Fly**

14. Three words to describe myself:**Loving, Cool, Humorous**

15. Favorite song: **I Got It (Pastor Mike Jr.)**

16. When is the last time you felt loved: **When I found God**

17. **Celebrity Crush? LaRoyce C. Hawkins**

18. Who is your hero? **Sophia Ruffin-Wilson**

19. What's your superpower? **Worship is my superpower**

20. If you became a millionaire tomorrow, what would be your first three purchases? **A Loft, A Rolls Royce, and A Basketball Court**

21. What is the strongest trait you want your future husband to have? **I want him to be an intercessor for the kingdom of God. He has to love God more than he loves me. He has to be emotionally mature. I want him to admire everything about me. He has to be trustworthy in action. He has to be able to make me laugh. He has to be willing to apologize TO ME when he's wrong. He has to be able to pick me up in the spirit and in the natural.**

22. Favorite NBA Team: **Boston Celtics**

23. **Favorite NBA player: Jayson Tatum**

24. Favorite WNBA team: **Las Vegas Aces**

25. Favorite WNBA player: **Maya Moore**

26. Biggest Fear: **Failure**

27. Favorite TV Show: **Sistas**

28. Favorite Actor: **Ryan Reynolds**

29. Favorite Actress: **Naturi Naughton**

30. Name something on your bucket list? **To go on a cruise**

Part Three

THIRD QUARTER

LIFE OUTSIDE THE PAINT

"A life without God is a lost game."

~Miriam Tamar Holmes

7

OUTSIDE SHOOTER

A player who takes shots from the perimeter.

Shooting the ball outside of the perimeter was one of my favorite things to do. I had a crossover like Sheryl Swoopes and a fade away like Reggie Miller. Once I became hot on the court, I was unstoppable! I was persistent, talented, wise, and capable of playing all positions. The accuracy and confidence that I had as a player gave me a shooter's mentality. I think greatness was my portion because I was always ready and prepared to shoot and I always stayed in proper posture: with my knees bent, elbows close to my body and my wrist cocked. I remained in the winning position regardless of what was going on in the game.

Knowing how to shoot the ball is a very important skill in basketball. While I was a pure shooter on the court, I figured out how to shoot my shot off the court as well. Even though being a rookie now playing for the other team was quite new for me, I didn't miss a shot. I was on fire from the very start of my indulgence in this newfound lifestyle. For every basket that I made, the confidence and self-assurance that each new experience gave me had me now assuming the position of the initiator in my encounters with other females. I was moving forward with an even greater stride than I'd ever had in any of my previous relationships with men. The way that I dressed, the way that I walked, the way that I talked, and even the way that my hair was styled gave off such a definitive masculine appearance and vibe that it was even scary to me. In the midst of living such a brazen lifestyle, I still feared God and I was deathly afraid of the person that I was becoming.

I was beyond confused at the individual that stared back at me in the mirror. Here I was: choosing to present myself in a masculine manner and I didn't even know why. I mean, I was already a tomboy. Someone asked me if I did anything else to downplay my femininity, but my response was that, unfortunately, I never felt that I had any! It was easy for me to go from baggy clothes to men's clothing, as it was a natural outgrowth of the lifestyle. I didn't want to be labeled, but people will begin to label you anyway, whether you like it or not…if you present yourself in a certain fashion. It made the transition in my appearance that much easier. I began to lose myself as a result of my lack of self control, and my heart became filled to the brim with lust. I was so far gone and distant from the person that my parents molded me to be.

I was living a "free" lifestyle at this point in my journey, and I was enjoying myself. My first sexual encounter with Queen had my mind blown. She made me feel like I was in a relationship with her. When I found out that she wasn't as serious as I was because of her own freedom and encounters with several other women, I had mixed emotions. Everything was new, and it hit me all at the same time. I had to own the fact that I went into things with Queen knowing that she already had someone. I couldn't be devastated behind what I already knew, so I just took it as one to grow on. Plus, I realized that Queen was just an "around the way girl" on the campus yard, and those facts helped me move forward as well. Now, I was open to all types of experiences.

There was so much going on in my life at this point, that I didn't think that there was anything left that could catch me by surprise! Despite this fact, I never would've imagined myself being a married man's secret! There were now all kinds of plot twists in my story, but the character that entered my relational "scene" at this time was a connection that was significant for many reasons. I thought I preferred women, and I also thought that I was now closed to the idea of sex with men.

"Mr. Parker" came into my world and shook things up in a way I wouldn't have expected in a million years!

I met Mr. Parker in passing on campus. Being that I was a person who wanted what I wanted with no strings attached, this was the ideal situation for me. Although I was rejected by a man when I was much younger, that still never pushed me away from intimate encounters with men. Being double-minded and unstable was not only an understatement, but it was truly what I had begun to embody. I enjoyed the fun times that Mr. Parker and I shared. Getting intoxicated and having freestyle rap battles started off as our favorite thing to do on the college campus and that was the extent of it at first. I never once gave into the thought that a man would want to be remotely interested sexually or any other kind of way in a woman who wore both the clothing and energy of a man **well**. I knew he was married, but he wasn't interested in my personal life and I wasn't interested in his either. It was the perfect setup from the pits of hell because he was the ideal "sneaky link" for me! Being under the influence of any drug or alcohol couldn't possibly make me feel the way he made me feel the very first time. With things being so unexpected, we never stopped to think about what was going on. I was just so shocked at the experience of his amazing foreplay and how he pulled down those men's boxers that I wore just like they were a pair of Victoria's Secret panties!

My encounters with "Mr. Parker" were so different, that his presence in my life ended up being more than a one-time fling. Whenever we were in public, we were like homies. He was my ninja and I was his ninja. Behind closed doors, it was a very different story. The overall chemistry was amazing…but the physical chemistry was far greater than words could describe. Whatever mode I was in, Mr. Parker knew how to handle me….whether it was speeding things up or taking things slow…and I didn't even have to tell him! Honestly, he had more faith in my ability to be a woman than I did.

When homosexuality knocked on my door, it felt so unreal to me the way everything (including my wardrobe) changed so rapidly. I was still so confused about what was happening to me as far as this same-sex lifestyle was concerned. In the midst of this confusion, Mr. Parker came in and almost seemed to begin to set things in order...as if there was any order, rhyme, or reason going on in my life at the time! Even after my first full experience with Queen, Mr. Parker brought me back and commenced to blow my mind and my body at a level that no man had ever come close to! I had never, ever had an orgasm with a man before, nor one at all before Queen. Remember, I had just started out on my sexual journey with females right before this juncture, and, in my opinion, there's nothing like your first orgasm. In case you're wondering: there was no comparison between Queen and Mr. Parker. The mere fact that my first orgasm was with a woman had been the key to opening that same-sex relationship door. However, encountering Mr. Parker had been one of the most pleasurable experiences I'd had in my life up to that **new** moment. He made me feel a thousand times greater in the way that he dealt with me with no strings attached. Is it wrong for me to keep it real right now as I write, remembering that Mr. Parker just simply had some **more than amazing, breathtakingly dumbfounding** sex as I try to describe our connection? (pray saints!)

No matter what most women go through, after a certain period of time when you are physically involved with someone, emotions will find a way to come into the picture. After some months went past, I called Mr. Parker up one night just to say those three powerful words: "I love you." For the first time, I heard nothing but anger in his voice as he told me to **never** say it again. For over a week, I didn't hear anything else from him. Eventually, he called me back, and the physical chemistry picked up right back where we'd left it…but now it was much more strong and intense. Although I understood his anger, going from no strings attached, no responsibility, and no accountability to me expressing my feelings for him was huge and unexpected. The feminine humanity on the inside of me always had a way of reminding me of who I was: a woman wearing men's clothing who was confused and unstable. This "thing" between Mr. Parker and I ended up lasting for a few years. Ironically, this was the placeholder I used to try my best not to completely cross over into a full-fledged lifestyle of homosexuality.

A double-minded man is unstable in all his ways. (James 1:8 [KJV])

8

FOUL BALL

A foul that is called on any player or coach who makes an illegal physical or verbal action against another player.

During a basketball game, if you reach a certain total of fouls, you will be put out of the game for exceeding the number of fouls permitted. Although there are different types of fouls in a basketball game, the personal foul was one to remember for me. Why? Fouls are an enormous part of any basketball game. A personal foul is the kind of foul that an *individual* player makes, but every type of foul affects the team. I was always that player who stayed on the court and in the game the majority of the time from beginning to end, so fouling out for me was not one of my signature moves. That being said, there were still times that I did foul out of a game. Fouling out was one of the worst and most helpless feelings in the world: having to sit the game out on the bench while your team is in trouble. My goal was to keep my opponents from scoring, but I ended up fouling out and sitting on the sidelines, unable to make a difference when and where it mattered most! If I had been more careful with the way that I handled my body, I would've still been in the game.

As I discussed in previous chapters, This first foul that I encountered was rejection and it was the stepping stone that walked me right into simultaneous seasons filled with unhealthy lifestyle choices. Oftentimes, God will remove those negative things and people from our lives when we are too attached, too inadequate, and too mindlessly blinded to see accurately. I would think to myself at times,

"Why was I rejected at a young age while I was too weak and powerless to handle a situation of that magnitude?" Now here I am living a foul life and completely out of the Will of God. I never thought I would be so far away from God. The enemy had me playing right into the palm of his hands. This foul was personal.

My college experience had gotten pretty wild pretty fast. I couldn't get a grip on the ball (my life) and this led me to my next loose ball foul. I lost possession of the ball and realized that the enemy had it the entire time! Through it all, God was still in control of the game. I couldn't comprehend God's grace for the life of me because I was living so deeply in my own grief and greed. I began to slowly lose interest in what I went to college for, which was to prepare for the future. I was uncertain about my life's plan before I got to college, but I knew that going to college would help me discover my career path and acquire a span of advanced knowledge in the specific areas that interested me the most. I also knew that being away from home was a considerable opportunity to take responsibility for myself and make my own decisions in life. So I battled throughout the school year trying to maintain possession of the ball...but the more I battled, the more I came in contact with a body...or *bodies*...and this cannot only make you lose your grip on the game, but reality altogether.

Fleshly temptation had gotten the best of me and had become part of a spiritual war that I was unable to fight and win. I didn't initiate the physical contact that came my way at first, but with same-sex experiences, things changed quickly. I knew in my heart of hearts that I needed to slow down before my sins caught up with me, but sex addiction and alcohol abuse had made it to the driver's seat of my life. I gained offensive fouls back-to-back because I was all over the place. I went from building to building and from dorm room to dorm room sleeping with any woman that wanted a good time. Some mornings I would wake up in my bed with a smile on my face and other times I would wake up in someone else's bed sick in disbelief wondering how I found my way in bed with someone that was so unattractive. Alcohol can truly bring out the beauty in a person until you get sober! After several nights of the same-ole, same-ole...I began to slow down and sober up at least for a moment to think about the direction my life was going in. One night, I got out a piece of notebook paper and wrote down a list of names of the men and women that I had slept with. Why did I do that? Those fouls seemed so unreal. As wild as this exercise was, looking back, I can still detect some growth in my decision to simply sit down and reflect on the road I was going down...because for a long time, I didn't know who I was or what was becoming of me. I knew that I had made so much intimate contact with so many people that I had completely fouled out of the game. I made contact with over 100 bodies in just a few years. I had lost many games...but I felt like I had lost my mind as well after making that list! I started to feel so convicted and ashamed. How do I go to God now? What can I possibly say to him?

Now, I'm failing in school and I have fouled out of the game. Honoring God in college can truly be the key to success. I was rejecting God and I didn't count up the cost. Are you currently living your life as you please? Are you doing the things that please man or God? Now is the time to come out from the shadows and get back in the game and be free. No one, whether they know it or not, wants to face the hardship of being rejected by God.

But Samuel replied, "What is more pleasing to the Lord: your burnt offerings and sacrifices or your obedience to his voice? Listen, Obedience is better than sacrifice, and submission is better than offering the fat of rams. Rebellion is as sinful as witchcraft, and stubbornness as bad as worshiping idols. So because you have rejected the commands of the Lord he has rejected you as king." (1 Samuel 15:22-23 [NLT])

9
FREE THROW

An unhindered shot in basketball made from behind a set line and awarded because of a foul by an opponent.

Shooting free throws in a game was truly my profession. Not to brag, but I was a goat at the free throw line. Why? One reason was because I knew how important free throws were in the grand scheme of the game. Do you know how excited people act when receiving something for free? Well, that was me at the free throw line, excited and always prepared in perfect form to shoot and make my shots. Free throws give you an additional opportunity to score, and they will also put the other team in jeopardy (in terms of fouls and points). The more shots you make at the free throw line, the better your chances are at winning the game. My main position in basketball was a power forward and it was my goal to make my opponents foul me. So I did my job, and I did it well. The game has begun and my moment of truth has come.

It is impossible to shoot any shot while sitting on the bench on the sidelines of the game. On the bench, there are no more fouls to give and no more free throws to make. My college years went left real fast. I thought that it was in my best interest to sit out for the next few semesters until I figured out the importance of my career. On one of those final days as I packed up and prepared to leave college, I walked past what I thought was the most beautiful girl in the world! She had completely gotten my attention. I stopped in the middle of the yard and I never took my eyes off her until she wasn't able to be seen anymore.

Even before leaving school, I looked for her day and night and always came up dry. After leaving school and never seeing her again, I was so excited when I happened to run across her on social media where I also learned what her name was. Let's call her Ivory. I sent her a friend request via Facebook and her acceptance was the beginning of an introduction that sent me head-over-heels. From the moment that I saw her, my thoughts, desires, and imaginations went to a wild side and a stronghold that I couldn't and didn't want to come out of. Everything that I was ever taught about God went straight out of the window. I wanted what I wanted and I didn't stop until I got it.

It all started from one simple inbox on Facebook and the conversation never ended until we met. Getting to know her was nothing short of amazing. I was always so comfortable talking to her. She stated that she had never talked to a masculine female before, but noted that it was something about me. Her curiosity led her from asking questions to wanting to engage physically in the same-sex lifestyle. So after a few months of communicating, I took a Megabus to Chicago to visit her for the first time. Things got serious pretty quickly. I went from visiting on a weekend to staying over for weeks at a time. It seemed things got serious enough for us to talk about moving in together almost instantly. This new found same-sex relationship with Ivory put me out of the game, and now I have completely settled down. It had been three months and twenty-five days since Ivory and I became a couple, and I'd never been so happy in my entire life! I didn't think I cared so much for love until I was with her and saw how her actions matched her words.

I knew things were very serious between Ivory and I, but what I didn't know was how serious she was until she initiated discussions about us having a child together. As she spoke, I processed things in silence...but after just a few minutes of thinking about her sentiments, I felt excitement and pure love at the thought of having a child and a family with her. I'd never been so weak-minded and yet, so full of happiness. This elation continued at the fact that I didn't have to actually go through labor to birth a child myself, but now I could still become a mother just the same. Starting a family with a woman was a real game changer. After only a few conversations about it, **she** made some things happen and **she** was pregnant before I moved in. Things were moving faster than I could even process them all at that time. Eventually, I moved in and life became a whirlwind! Just like that, we had a family with two amazing boys that she had from a previous relationship, and now we had <u>our</u> baby boy! She gave him a name that meant "God is with us".

This baby boy truly lived up to his name, because God was with him all the way. He was and is a miracle child that I had fallen in love with from the moment that I laid eyes on him. After Ivory had our son, the love she and I shared grew stronger and stronger with each passing day. With a bond like this, the looming question became "How would it ever be possible to break away from this lifestyle and even attempt to be free?" How could I ever live life minus the person that I felt like I could never again live without?

It was 12-12-12. This triple-digit date will only fall once in a lifetime. What an unbelievable day it was! I remember having a conversation with her the day before about the upcoming date and she said something like: "Let's make an amazing memory tomorrow!" The request that she made next literally blew me away! Marriage?!? I mean, I was truly happy with the state of my relationship. She was the love of my life and I **did** want to share every part of my existence with her. Being with her just felt right. At that point, I couldn't imagine life without her. I lived to make her happy, but for some reason, I couldn't shake the things my parents taught me.

Honestly, the twelve years that I had lived an alternative lifestyle still never made marrying a woman feel like the right thing for me to do. Less than 24 hours later, I couldn't believe that we were headed to Iowa to get a same-sex marriage license! I was a nervous wreck, but I'd never felt love like this before in my entire life. This love was unconditional, everlasting, and authentic. It was strong enough to make me get out of the car and walk up to the courthouse door…

During this time, same-sex marriage was only legal in a few states…and the closest state to Chicago that recognized same-sex marriage was Iowa. That day, a three-and-a-half hour drive felt like a nerve-wracking two whole days! The entire trip, every single thing my parents taught me about God started to surface in my head, threatening to drive me mad. All I wanted to do in my heart was to make her happy. I was so caught up in our happiness that I didn't think about how marrying her felt like a straight shot to hell until the road trip that day. Every sin that I had ever done came rushing back to me like the billboards I was passing as we rode down the highway. The time that was supposed to be the happiest moment of my life turned into pure conviction from God. I felt so sick, ashamed, and full of anxiety at the thought of judgment and the knowledgeable awareness of hell's fire.

What Ivory and I felt that day was completely different, and I wasn't honest enough to share it with her. Even in the middle of my convictions - I still wanted her to be happy. I still wanted her to feel the same love that she had given me in return. I still wanted to feel the love that I had been running from for so many years. God knew the plans that He had for me, but the love that I felt for Ivory made me too weak to stand up to the truth in the moment or fight back. So, on 12-12-12, I pushed through every conviction and fear to get a same-sex marriage license to become lawfully wedded to Ivory.

We drove back to Chicago that night in celebration of being one. As much as I wanted to feel the happiness that she was feeling, I couldn't shake the brokenness of how mindful and aware I was of the sinful guilt God had shown me and how He allowed me to feel conviction again (though I still dishonored him)! I was truly happy with the love that Ivory and I shared, but the fear of God started to creep up within me day in and day out like never before. At times it was so hard to enjoy life with her because God wouldn't let me rest. I never wanted her to think that I wasn't happy, because I was. It's just that God's conviction will override the joy of willful sin every time.

And when he comes, he will convict the world of its sin, and of God's righteousness, and of the coming judgment. (John 16:8 [NLT])

TIME-OUT

LET'S PRAY

Lord, create in me a clean heart and renew a right Spirit within me. Build my faith in your strength and answer my prayers as they wholeheartedly align to your will. Give me the holy boldness to speak the word of God and to resist the devil and his tricks and schemes. Remove any words and actions motivated by fear and uncertainty from my arsenal. Remove the scales from my eyes that seek to cloud the vision that you've placed in my heart.

Lord, close every door of disobedience so that the spirit of righteousness can awaken within me. I want to carry out your will for my life. I rebuke every spirit of homosexuality that seeks to destroy my mind, body, and soul. Any destructive spirit that would try to lead me toward the pits of hell through adultery and fornication, you are defeated in Jesus's name. God, please continue to give me the strength to crucify the flesh so that I can recover, heal, and be set free from the homosexual lifestyle. Holy Spirit, fortify my life so that it may line up with God's word.

Lord, I have confessed my sexual sins and I ask that you will place them under your blood. May the fire of God burn every sexual desire and appetite that's not pleasing to you. Take away the yearning desire for what is forbidden and all that goes against your word. I break every soul tie with men and women that I have had sexual relations with. Lord, please forgive me for yielding my body to this lifestyle. I repent for living a life of lesbianism, rebellion, adultery and fornication. Please forgive me for transgressing against your word and my own body. Set me free from every bondage of sin. I thank you for my freedom and my healing. Have your way in me, In Jesus mighty Name, Amen.

Part Four

FOURTH QUARTER

THE GAME CHANGER

"Work hard in stillness, crossover with a roar."

~Miriam Tamar Holmes

10

HOME COURT ADVANTAGE

The physical and psychological benefits that a player experiences when competing in his own arena/area.

The benefit of home court advantage is having comfort in knowing that you are home with family and friends rather than being on the road. Being at home doesn't always guarantee you a win, but it is unquestionably an advantage. I always had a next-level turn up when I would hear the support of the crowd going wild at home. Just to hear someone cheering for you on the sidelines definitely had a way of motivating you to play your best. Home court advantage didn't just affect me, it affected the team. It gave us a level of confidence and the motivation that we needed to win.

After Ivory and I became one and started a family together, we decided to make a big move for the safety of our family and start a new life in a new state with new opportunities. Things were going so amazingly great in our relationship at this time. We did everything together! Ivory was the first one to find a job, and I stayed home to take care of the three boys. It was a learning experience for me to take care of two young boys and a newborn baby, but the more I learned, the greater the connection got. I was graced with the opportunity and honor to raise and get to know some amazing children. I even got a chance to see the baby boy take his first steps. As he walked for the first time, he had a laughter and a joy inside of him that was so hearty, that he would topple over! Our home was filled with love and laughter. The emotions and everything else that I felt inside as a mother and wife were unexplainable. Despite everything, those were unforgettable memories that I will forever cherish.

As time went by, I was blessed with a job and we were able to send the kids off to school and daycare. Things were finally looking up for my family and I. It felt as if God's conviction had passed over. I was restful, at peace, and happy as a fat squirrel in a nut factory. We were both living our best life. Despite all of my knowledge of God and His goodness, I continued to live in sin. I became way too comfortable living life on a sinful path. I had gotten to the point where I was completely deaf to the voice of God. I learned the hard way that if we keep resisting God, eventually He will speak to us and we will not hear Him. Happiness that isn't ordained by God will cost you eternal freedom, and I have always been in fear of that even when I willfully lived in my sin. The Bible states in Matthew 13:13," Therefore I speak to them in parables, because seeing they do not see, and hearing they do not hear, nor do they understand." With me not seeing nor hearing, I thought that

I was at the point of no return with God. How selfish am I, resisting God but not wanting him to resist me?

Oftentimes, I would go back home to Mississippi to visit my parents. The advantages of being at home were a complete understatement when it came to my family. They always loved me unconditionally in spite of me and my shortcomings. During one of my stays while visiting home, I ran across an old family friend whom I hadn't seen or heard from in a while. Let's call her Snow. She didn't know I was living in Georgia at the time, which was also where she resided as well. So after a short conversation, she invited me to come to church with her once we were both back home in Atlanta. It took me some time to think about it, but eventually I went to visit one Sunday morning. I really enjoyed myself! After the first visit, Snow invited me to come back the following Sunday and asked me to bring my family with me as well. There were two well-known facts that Ivory and I shared and that was us having a love for God and the fact that we both loved church. So I went home to tell Ivory about the amazing time I had at church and I also shared with her the invitation that I got to come the following Sunday but this time with my entire family. I found comfort the very first time I went to church. They were serious about God, they were loving, and they welcomed me with open arms. That was the open door and the divine connection that God had lined up for my life. Just when I thought that God had completely rejected me, He sent someone to provide guidance, love, and godly knowledge. The evidence of God's calling was back in my life-but this time it was stronger than ever! There was something about GOD calling me this time and in this season that I couldn't seem to shake.

My family and I started to make going to church a priority in our home. We were all excited about church on Sundays and even sometimes going to Bible study during the week. We weren't just going because of the enjoyment. There was some real praise and real worship going on in our home, with Ivory and even the boys joining in. The catch was that now, I had come right back to the place where I was having those same convictions regarding my lifestyle that began hitting my mind like a ton of bricks once again. During Sunday worship services, the presence of God would always be so heavy in church. Eventually, I would begin to weep and cry out for God. So many times when I began to cry, I didn't even know why I was crying.

All I knew is that God was doing a new thing in me. There were times that we would arrive home from church and yet take a few shots of alcohol, have a few beers, and even have sex. How could I be free from such a lifestyle when I'm coming back home to it? See, I began to realize that my church life wasn't matching my home life and that began to feel like a problem for me. I had straddled the fence on both sides...but not WITH God. So we continued churching and literally **OUT OF THE BLUE** there was a shaking in our home, in our relationship, and in our finances! There were definitely arguments in the past, but this time hurricane Katrina, Isaac, and Irene couldn't compare to the turmoil going on in our home and in our lives!

Fast forward, we were marked safe in the midst of this unbelievable turmoil....but God wasn't finished yet! One Sunday, the pastor called a 3 day Daniel Fast. This was a special event for the church, and this was both me and Ivory's first time ever going on a fast. It was literally the hardest three days of my life, especially since I was shacking up with someone. Plus, in the midst of God shaking things up in our home, he also shook some things up in the system as well. I came to find out that our same-sex marriage license was **VOIDED**!

God was moving behind the scenes in such a supernatural way that I couldn't even comprehend it all! On that very last day of the Daniel Fast, I remember being home alone and there was a breakthrough that took place in my life. I began to pray like never before, I went into a praise like never before, and tongues in other languages began to flow from my belly out of my mouth that I had never heard before. I was so scared, but at that very moment, I felt a hunger for God at a maximum level!

Ivory and I had our bad days and we had our good days, but the bad days were beginning to outweigh the good days as God continued the shaking in our home. Sooner rather than later, I made a decision to walk away from my job and my family. I remember waiting until the boys went to sleep because I didn't want to see the look on their faces when I turned my back to walk out of their lives for good. That night was one of the worst days of my life. The brokenness I felt was indescribable. I caught the next Greyhound bus back home to Mississippi. I cried the whole entire trip home in disbelief at what God was doing in my life. In that moment, it felt like God had just taken away the only thing that I found comfort, peace, and joy in. Our relationship was what I called my "happy place". She was the love of my life, but she was also my first-class ticket to hell. Even in sin, I still feared God and had the wisdom enough to know that I wasn't going to hell for nobody. So, yes I would rather lose her than to lose my soul.

For I know the thoughts that I think towards you, says the Lord, thoughts of peace and not of evil, to give you a future and a hope. Then you will call upon Me and go and pray to Me, and I will listen to you. And you will seek Me and find Me, when you search for Me with all your heart. I will be found by you, says the Lord, and I will bring you back from your captivity; I will gather you from all the nations and from all the places where I have driven you, says the Lord, and I will bring you to the place from which I cause you to be carried away captive. (Jeremiah 29:11-14 [NKJV])

11

FULL COURT PRESS

A defensive tactic in which the defense applies pressure to the offensive team the entire length of the court.

In a basketball game, a "full court press" is a defensive strategy that is well known and often used in the heat of the game. This tactic is most often employed when the game is extremely close and an intense defense against the opposing team is required. Guarding a player one-on-one the full length of the court was not for the weak. So while putting pressure on the offense, the pressure was yet and still on the defense as well. Why? The defense wants to put so much force on the ball that the offensive team loses it or ends up turning the ball over. Full court press is suffocating and it can cause the offensive team to lose their sense of direction.

Sometimes we don't realize the strength of the aggression that the enemy has put in place against our lives until it's too late. In basketball, we use the full court press tactics at certain times...but in life, we should *always* use this defensive mechanism against the enemy. When I walked away from my family to live a life pleasing to God, the enemy tried to press, threaten, and even terrorize me...trying to convince me that I made the wrong decision. My flesh was still weak, and my heart was still broken. At first, I didn't know how to submit or surrender my all to God. In my mind, it was both devastating and disorienting to try to learn how to live a life without the love of my life or our boys! I couldn't think past "go". I was sick with a lack of motivation, a loss of appetite, episodes of rage, and a one track mind that only consisted of Ivory alongside heavy shortness of breath! I constantly thought, "God, how can I possibly serve you in this condition?"

I had to face some hard truths that teased and taunted me right next to my desire to live right. I mean, I wouldn't have left my home and family for nothing and no one else but God! I didn't fully understand what was happening to me, but all I knew was that I chose God. I had so many questions as to why I was struggling so hard to submit. Was it really even possible for someone who had experienced what I had gone through to live for Christ while still in love with a woman? How could I resist the devil with the weight of this lifestyle still so heavy upon me? What was I supposed to do about my sexual appetite and even my desires now that I was no longer living *like* a married woman?

Being without Ivory had me completely anxious and under some major pressure. I literally didn't know how to live without sex or Ivory, but I knew that I couldn't disobey God or go back. I tried so hard to stay focused and to keep my mind on God, but I didn't have the discernment to acknowledge the enemy's schemes and I didn't think that I had the authority to defeat him. I wasn't strong enough to stand in the face of the enemy. The devil was seeking to destroy me the second that I made it back home. I was in a losing battle against the full court press of temptation all because the devil knew my weakness and I played right into his hands.

In the midst of my struggle, I ran across someone who had always been near and dear to my heart. We made conversation and that conversation led to visitation. I thought I was strong enough to be able to enjoy a simple conversation and boy was I wrong. Unbelievably, I found myself back in bed having sex with a woman *once again*. I didn't understand for the life of me what was going on. I knew a change had come, but somehow my life still looked and felt the same. It is a strong tactic of the enemy to make us think that just because we struggle in the time of our transition from darkness to light, that we are still bound by our old habits. The truth is, the weakest new Christian is stronger than the devil if they have a repentant heart and rely on the authority of God's word to defeat the tactics of the enemy! The word of God says in 2nd Corinthians 12:9 that God's strength is made perfect in our weakness, and I was weaker than wet tissue. I knew enough to know that help was available, and I knew *just* where I needed to go to get it!

I started going back to church in my hometown because I knew that God brought me back home for a reason. The closer I got to God, the more the enemy fought me. I developed a mega-hunger and thirst after righteousness because I wanted to be ten steps ahead of the enemy at all times. For that reason, I became active in the kingdom of God. Not only was I attending Sunday services, I also started to attend bible study as well, and did whatever it took to get close to God and to His people. There is strength in numbers, and it really did help me to be around true saints of God.

After worshiping regularly and serving God faithfully, some things started to change. I begin to learn more about God's plan for my life. One of the first things that changed was how I developed a deep and abiding trust in God. I was used to relying on the kind of intimacy that involved other willing human participants that helped me feed my flesh. Yet, here I was...alone and relearning how to walk with God. I had to learn how to lean SOLELY on God's grace. I cried through many nights feeling the sting of loneliness and feeling literally heartbroken. The strength that came out of this season became the catalyst to transform my depression into praise. I wasn't just praising God when times were good, I praised him in difficult times as well.

Every Sunday at the end of church service, I found myself at the altar. At times, I would be in fear because I knew something was happening to me and that I wasn't in control anymore. I still had an appearance of masculinity and I still dressed myself in men's clothing. People would always look and stare at me as if I was still in the lifestyle. People would talk to and around me as if I was still in the lifestyle. The more I pressed in prayer, the more

God began to deliver me from the opinion of other people. After a while, it was just like no one was there but me and God! If I needed to go to the altar every Sunday, I did. If I needed to weep and cry out to God during Sunday morning worship, I did. I didn't stop until I was free. I still wore men's boxers, but my soul was free. I was still in men's clothing, but my spirit was free. I was still wearing men's cologne, but on the inside of me I was free. People will judge you by your outer appearance, yet have no clue what God is doing on the inside!

So if the Son sets you free, you will be free indeed. (John 8:36 (NLV])

12

CROSSOVER

A way of faking out other basketball players by rapidly switching the ball from one hand to the other and changing direction of travel.

The crossover is one of the most commonly utilized moves in the game of basketball. It is one of the premier ways to maintain control of the ball when pressure is put on you by members of the other team. As long as your control skills are great, you have the ability to move freely and change directions on the court as you please. In order to precisely execute a crossover move, you have to know how to handle the ball. Handling the ball is a very important skill on the court, especially for the point guard. Playing ball in my youth, I would always visualize myself having a crossover like Allen Iverson. No matter how hard I practiced, I never seemed to get his moves down to a science - but I certainly had a few moves of my own.

Crossing over from the lifestyle of homosexuality has been one of my greatest moves of all time! That move shook my opponents to their ankles and left them in a state of shock. It took more than just physical practice to make this move. To be honest, it wasn't easy at all, but I was so extremely hungry for God. To go from being a sex addict to practicing celibacy felt like a nightmare! The awareness of going from a nympho to a nun has, at times, felt like torture at its highest peak and made me feel like I had received a life sentence in prison! My legs have truly been locked up with a maximum sentence until this very day…but there will be parole after marriage, lol!!!! Endeavoring to come out of homosexuality is a battle that you have to pray and prepare to overcome.

Freedom is not just a destination, but a journey that continues throughout one's lifetime. In order to win your freedom back from the enemy, you have to learn how to make serious sacrifices. To walk away from a same-sex lifestyle heavily involves crucifying, or killing (through IGNORING) the flesh. My flesh was weaker than weak, and the only thing that I knew that would bring me out was to develop a habit of consecration. To consecrate means to give yourself to God through the frequent practice(s) of fasting, praying, bible reading and studying, listening to and feeding my spirit with songs of praise & worship and hearing/meditating on the preached Word of God. All of these activities, when utilized consistently, enable one to go from a life that is led by fleshly desires, to a life of focus in a way where your body actually becomes the "living sacrifice." A living sacrifice is what is left over of someone after their old way of living is surrendered to God. It should be such a significant change that a surrendered life brings...so much so that one begins to look, sound, and even appear to literally be a whole new person. The change should be evident in motivation, conversation, desires, and behavior. I wasn't just seeking deliverance, I needed the strength, knowledge, and understanding of how to stay and walk in my deliverance. So I began to consecrate, fast, and pray like there was no tomorrow. The stronger I got in God, the more the enemy came for my life.

At a certain point, I started to second-guess myself as to whether I was really saved or not. Oftentimes, I would look at myself in the mirror and I would see the same person on the *outside*. I knew without a doubt in my mind that God had done a new thing in me, but the enemy wanted me to think otherwise. I questioned the validity of my deliverance. Even before I came to Christ, I always felt that it would be impossible to change how I looked or carried myself on the outside. For so long, I appeared to myself and everyone else in the form of a masculine woman. So I started to speak to God in prayer concerning my outer appearance. God loves us and He wants to hear from us, we just need to know how to pray according to His will.

The Bible says in Mark 11:24, *Therefore I tell you, whatever you ask for in prayer, believe that you have received it, and it will be yours.* One of my initial prayers was short and simple, and it went like this: **"Lord, here I am asking you to help me make changes on the outside so that my appearance will line up with the works that you have done on the inside of my heart. Let what I thought was impossible manifest to be possible and visible to others and even to me. In Jesus's name, Amen."**

God helped me make major moves in this game, I just needed the right coach to assist me as I *fully* crossed over. I was tired of losing and was ready to really WIN! Sometime in 2016, I ended up joining this live video streaming app called Periscope. I know that in my God-given discernment that it was not by any coincidence that I ran across this bold, loud, and amazing lady by the name of Sophia Ruffin giving her testimony. No matter what people had to say, she freely told her story without fear every time she went live. I couldn't believe what I was hearing because our testimonies were so similar. She was truly God-sent to so many people across the nation, but I knew beyond a shadow-of-a-doubt that she was sent especially to me! After following her for some time, I began to learn so many things concerning my transformation and other issues that I had been praying about. I felt so alone going through my journey until I started following her.

Up to that point, I had never met anyone else that had been so deep in the homosexual experience but who had now submitted their *entire* lifestyle to God. I knew through her deliverance that I definitely wasn't alone. Later on, I listened to her story about how she transformed from a masculine female through a process she called [1]***Feminine Progression***, which became the title of one of her books. She was uplifting and encouraging, and she became my biggest inspiration.

My own journey toward femininity was similar to Sophia's, but also very different in many ways. One of my most profound moments of transition occurred when I was directly confronted regarding my "masculinity." I met a friend of a friend one day, and all three of us were in conversation. Eventually, we became friends too. Not many days afterward, she called me and said that she wanted to ask me a question. I told her "sure" as I was interested in what she had to say. She asked me if she was correct in thinking that I had on men's cologne. I told her "yes." She went on to ask me why. The truth was, I didn't even have an answer to give her, because I didn't even know!

I had become so used to waking up, putting on my boxer shorts, putting on male clothing and cologne that it had become a habit. Her question shook me to my core! Yes, God had begun the work of transformation within, but I didn't realize that I was STILL moving in what was **familiar** to me…walking around still looking and smelling like a man. I was literally ashamed.

Speaking of **familiarity**, it was so hard to break free from the pull of ungodliness that kept me tied up in my sinful addictions. The familiar spirit is a demon of bondage that seeks to keep all of God's children from healing and deliverance. This spirit seeks to remove God from His throne in our hearts and lives. In order to keep those doors unable to be opened by the enemy, we have to be truthful to God about our struggles. Someone might wonder *"How do I know that I'm under attack by a familiar spirit?"* You know you are under an attack from a familiar spirit when you know it's wrong, but it STILL feels like HOME!

Whenever we are more acquainted with these spirits and struggles than we are with having the desire to read, know and understand the Word of God-it is one of the clearest signs that we are in bondage or heading in that direction and need to turn and run **quickly**! A life of bondage and slavery to sin can happen in an instant whenever we begin to live life in an unaware state. Before we can break free from the familiar spirit, we have to be able to recognize and acknowledge that we are in a bad place. We cannot be in denial about where we really are, because denial is one of the greatest obstacles that stand in the way of change.

I was still going through the motions, carrying myself in masculine form. I had spent over half of my life stuck in this negative behavior pattern that I was not able to break free from. I had not yet discovered how to embrace my God-given identity. I was driving down a dead-end road, until I opened my heart and began to obey God. To be free from the familiar requires courage to OBEY. So let's make a STRONG decision to obey God, and ask Him to break the chains of bondage and sin off of us that the enemy brought to our doorstep and be free once and for all, in Jesus Mighty Name!

I thank God that He used my friend to call and question me regarding my walk with God and how it *appeared* that I was not representing Christ in the way I presented myself to the world. After turning our conversation over and over in my mind for several days, I ended up pressing past my fears and going to Walmart on a mission. I walked inside of the automatic double doors moving rapidly down the aisle towards the women's department to get some panties. I guessed my size, grabbed a pack of granny drawls, and literally ran to the cash register! I felt so embarrassed for some reason. Why??? I guess it was because it felt just as awkward as a straight male would have felt if he had to shop in the women's department, because I had never, ever shopped in the women's department as an adult! Also, I hadn't worn a pair of panties in over fifteen years. When I put those colorful women's underwear on, I think it was more of a declaration to the enemy than I even knew at the time. Honestly, I wasn't exactly happy about it, but it was truly God now moving and working on me like never before…making changes on both the inside and finally, the outside as well!

Immediately, I began feeling God's conviction in even more areas of my life. One evening, I went into my bedroom and just started throwing away all the boxer shorts I owned. Then, I began to pack up all of the male clothing and put it in a big garbage bag to give away. I must have gotten a cleaning bug in the natural AND in the spirit too, because what I did next literally shocked me! There was a bag of dumb dildos that I would keep in the trunk of my car (just in case). Thinking about it now, keeping them was actually a form of holding on to the past and making space in my life and behavior for my fleshly desires to be satisfied at some point [see Roman 13:14]. I took that bag of hot dogs to a nearby dumpster and tossed the bag in and didn't look back! God was moving in a mighty way! He was purging me past my own permissions so that I could please Him!

I talked to one of my church leaders at the time and told her that I was ready to go shopping for women's clothes. She was so excited for me, and she got me and another young lady from the church together and we went to the mall to shop for the beginnings of a new, more feminine wardrobe! At first, I didn't like how many outfits looked hanging on the rack, and I especially didn't care for the way I felt that they looked on my body. I was not used to actually having to face my female frame in the mirror, or seeing Miriam and all of her curves and girly glory...because my usual menswear would always keep me covered up. It truly felt kinda strange that day, and many days after that! I might have even worked my leaders' nerves a little because I hadn't developed my own style...and therefore, I didn't like much of anything she or the other young lady picked out for me. I was very grateful for their time and encouragement, as they continued to help me as I did eventually ease my way into a few flat shoe styles, some skinny jeans, and a Christian T-Shirt here and there. Give or take a blazer, and you have one of my signature looks to this day.

My brother Octavius was the one who helped push my desire to both look and feel feminine to another level. He had the amazing idea to give me a makeover and a photo shoot as a birthday present for my 35th birthday. He did such a phenomenal job styling me! Surprisingly, it did not feel awkward AT ALL to me that day. I had never in my entire life felt as beautiful as he made me feel at that moment. I felt NORMAL and I felt FEMININE...not as one that was trying to BE feminine...but as a WOMAN who had finally stepped into an acknowledgment of who I truly am. Here in plain sight staring at me from a mirror was this beautiful young woman that God had both called and made me to be from the foundation of the world at my core! I was so happy to finally see her emerge from her shell. The clothing designs were effortless...like someone had made each outfit he picked out especially for me. It was a boost to both my self-confidence and my self-esteem. It was as if God Himself ushered me into another season in the 35th year of my life because I could feel something new and refreshing happening to me....and I could see myself transforming before my very own eyes!

After my birthday fashion shoot, I started to step my game up appearance-wise. I did a makeup tutorial class, three more photo shoots, and I even went to a banquet at my church! For the banquet, I not only got my makeup done, but I also wore a dress AND some five-inch heels (bad idea wearing those....the strap broke and I almost fell, lol)!

Things all around me were changing, and I was beginning to embrace these changes in every way. It almost seemed as if everything in my life was synced up and coming together like a song being sung in perfect harmony. Although it literally felt as if the enemy was *still* watching me, I kept my eyes focused on God.

In this season, my friend circle changed. My habits changed. I was growing in the knowledge of the Word of God. My prayer life was increasing. I was constantly reading my bible. I was fasting with a group and being held accountable by other like-minded Christians and friends. I was in church all of the time. My parents kept me encouraged in my faith. I was even taking my nieces to church with me and watching God move in amazing ways in their lives as well.

I began to follow in the firm footsteps of my mentor, Sophia Ruffin, and began to make positive declarations over my life and even over my future and my destiny! Declarations are words, phrases, and sentences often accompanied by God's Word that are designed to steer your life in the direction of your positive expectations. The Bible declares that we are snared by the words of our mouth (*Proverbs 6:2 NIV*), so if we could talk ourselves <u>out</u> of some things, I knew most certainly that I could talk myself into some of the blessings and goodness that God has stored up for those who believe! It was my obedience that moved me closer and closer to Him. Through a war of words with the enemy whispering negativity in my ear, I spoke the Word of God on purpose over my life and prayed myself right into the Presence of the ALMIGHTY GOD!

I learned that there is no place on earth better than the Presence of God. Feeling His love and acceptance over my life has been the best and safest feeling I have ever felt in my entire life. His Presence changed me. Layers of wrong thoughts and desires I'd held on to for years began to fall off of my life like leaves on the trees in September. I began to ask God to lead and guide me instead of making all my plans for my life myself. I knew that I would never, ever be the same again. As my faith continued to grow, I began to rehearse specific declarations and affirmations over my life. Even when the enemy would try to laugh and mock me, I was, still am, and will continue to be steadfast, unmovable, and always abiding in God's goodness and in His love (*1 Corinthians 15:58a*). I'm on my way to heaven and I'm learning more every day about how to enjoy the journey.

As the songwriter said, He has rescued my life and I'm never going back. I am FREE, praise the Lord, I'm free. No longer bound... no more chains holding me. My soul is resting. It's just a blessing. Praise the Lord, Hallelujah, I'm free. Miriam Tamar Holmes is a beautiful young woman who is FINALLY FREE! I'm FULL OF FAITH and moving FORWARD into my FUTURE and my destiny, and FREEDOM feels and looks so good on me!

Therefore if any man be in Christ, he is a new creature: old things are passed away; behold, all things are become new (2 Corinthians 5:17 [KJV])

---

1. ***Feminine Progression***: *A process coined by International author and speaker Sophia Ruffin-Wilson that describes the process with which she went from a masculine-looking female (stud) after her salvation/conversion experience to looking and dressing in a more feminine manner...and one that matched her God-given, birth sex and newly-discovered identity.*

OVERTIME WINNING AFFIRMATIONS

FROM THE MVP..

I declare that I will *crossover* and be free from the spirit of rejection

·

I declare that I will *crossover* from rebellion to righteousness.

·

I declare that I will *crossover* and be delivered from the spirit of homosexuality

·

I declare that I will *crossover* into God's promises which is yes and Amen for me because I am in Christ

·

I declare that I will **crossover** from being the underdog to being unstoppable in Christ.

I declare that my weapons in Christ will have the divine power to destroy strongholds.

I declare that sin will have no dominion over me.

I declare that my mind, my body, and my soul will be cleansed of all lustful desires.

I declare that every generational curse that's hanging over my life will be supernaturally broken.

I declare that I am blessed coming in and blessed going out. (Deut. 28:6)

I declare that I can do all things through Christ who strengthens me. (Phill. 4:13)

I declare that I will not fear, because God is with me. (Is. 41:10)

I declare that the spirit of God dwells in me. (Corin. 5:7)

I declare that I will resist the devil and he will flee from me. (James 4:7)

I declare that I will **crossover** and be free.

FOOTNOTE CITATIONS

Merriam-Webster's Collegiate Dictionary (10th ed.). (1999). Merriam-Webster Incorporated.

Ruffin, Sophia. (2017). <u>Feminine Progression: How I Walked Out of Masculinity</u>. Life to Legacy Publishers, LLC

King James Bible. (2017). King James Bible Online. https://www.kingjamesbibleonline.org/

The Bible. Various Versions. *Bible Gateway*, version 42, Bible Gateway / Zondervan, 2016 https://www.biblegateway.com/

www.ingramcontent.com/pod-product-compliance
Lightning Source LLC
Chambersburg PA
CBHW051101160426
43193CB00010B/1270